Finding Jesus
in the
Dish Room

SCHUYLER VOWELL

ISBN 978-1-64028-106-6 (Paperback)
ISBN 978-1-64028-107-3 (Digital)

Copyright © 2017 by Schuyler Vowell
All rights reserved. No part of this publication may be reproduced, distributed, or transmitted in any form or by any means, including photocopying, recording, or other electronic or mechanical methods without the prior written permission of the publisher. For permission requests, solicit the publisher via the address below.

Christian Faith Publishing, Inc.
296 Chestnut Street
Meadville, PA 16335
www.christianfaithpublishing.com

Printed in the United States of America

Headshot by Nolan Winbun
Cover design by Cody Barger

The Holy Bible, English Standard Version® (ESV®)
Copyright © 2001 by Crossway,
a publishing ministry of Good News Publishers.
All rights reserved.
ESV® Text Edition: 2016

The Message (MSG)
Copyright © 1993, 1994, 1995, 1996, 2000, 2001, 2002 by Eugene H. Peterson.

Scripture quotations taken from the Amplified® **Bible (AMP),** Copyright © 2015 by The Lockman Foundation
Used by permission. www.Lockman.org"

Lord, I give you praise for who you are and for what you have already done. God, I thank you that it does not matter what our background is, the cross is what matters. God, I pray that as people read this, you would breathe on this, because without you, we have nothing. I pray that your grace would be all over this; I pray that you would open up eyes that have not seen you for who you really are. I pray that you would lift the heads of the discouraged and remind people that you—the creator of the universe, the savior of the world—are for us and not against us. Lord, I speak life, I speak hope into the weary souls today. In Jesus's name, and everybody said... Amen.

This book is dedicated to my Lord and Savior Jesus Christ, without your guidance, none of this would be possible. Even though I constantly fail, you love me immensely.

Contents

Acknowledgments 9

Foreword..11

Introduction..15

So Who is Jesus?..21

God the Father?...26

No Way, Hosea..30

Listen to your Heart?..35

Does God Have a Plan for Me? 39

Even If You Sleep with Your General's Wife, Get Her Pregnant, and then Have Him Killed, God Still Loves You 46

All Me 53

Girls Like Smoothies 60

Scandalous Grace 66

The Gospel Pep Talk 73

God, Can You Hear Me? 77

The Carpenter and the Crook 81

Even When You're Laying on Your Couch Alone, and Broke in the West End on Thanksgiving, God is Still Good 87

Is Jesus in Your Boat? 90

Selling God 95

Finding Jesus in the Dish Room 98

Acknowledgments

Thanks Jesus for inspiring me and having my back through this process.

Thanks Mama and Ned for your prayers.

Thanks Dad for believing in me.

Thanks Dustin for your friendship.

Thanks Amy for feeding me and letting me sleep on your futon.

Thanks Ms. Amburgy for your help.

Thanks Dr. Rose for your encouragement.

Thanks squad for believing in a twenty-year-old kid who sleeps on his mom's couch and makes burritos to lead you and thank you for stepping out of the boat with me.

Foreword

Schuyler Vowell has penned a rare gem. Not only is it notably humorous, but also it is the kind of raw, authentic Christian truth missing in the world today. The book is full of wit and wisdom, with a millennial world-view of cutting edge reason that's sure to entertain. More than anything, this book is an every man's journey on the sometimes long and winding road to redemption. "Finding Jesus in the Dish Room" is a must read for anyone searching for the truth and struggling to find God or wrestling with being real in expressing the love of God, to our lost and dying world.

Much is being made of the term "Relevant Christianity" these days. What does that term mean and what does it have to do with our world today? The timeless truth of the Living and Abiding Word of God is unchangeable. But, the way someone lives out that truth, is what makes it relevant to our world today. What good is it to have the truth and not have it received? Schuyler's book strikes a rare balance between immutable truth and cultural relevancy.

I first met Schuyler Vowell as he came walking down the hallway at the Corner of Hope Recovery Center, located in downtown Louisville, KY. I worked as the Clinical Director for a men and women's Rehabilitation Center, at the time. Schuyler strolled in to announce to me that he would be staying upstairs in our transitional living facility and wanted to help out in ministry. I found him engaging and his enthusiasm compelling. He was working as a dishwasher at a restaurant before making his way to Louisville to attend Bible College. He had a dream and goal to become an Ordained Minister and become a "voice of one crying in the wilderness" to an emerging feckless generation. I supported him then in his endeavors, as I certainly do now. Rev. Schuyler Vowell, continues to reach for the stars.

At the Corner of Hope Recovery Center, there was never a shortage of ministry opportunities. Almost daily, some type of ministry emergency would arise. Schuyler was always willing to jump into the fray, putting himself on the front-line to honestly and genuinely minister to those struggling to find hope. In Hebrews 6:19 AMP it states, "This hope [this confident assurance] we have as an anchor of the soul [it cannot slip and it cannot break down under whatever pressure bears upon it]—a safe and steadfast hope that enters within the veil [of the heavenly temple, that most Holy Place in which the very presence of God dwells]." The testimony of Schuyler Vowell is that hope has been a constant anchor for his soul and he has become a prognosticator for the awaiting hope anyone can find in Jesus.

When our ministry began to conduct homeless outreaches out into the deeper parts of the Inner-City of Louisville, Schuyler again volunteered himself to be used in this capacity. We would feed hundreds, on any given week and the opportunities for ministry were great. Every week we would see the disaffected, drug addicted, alcoholic, homeless, those in such suffering and despair, that their hope was fading fast. Schuyler drew upon his "Dish Boy Hope" and met people where they were, because the struggle is very real for those who believe God may have forgotten them.

Many mornings, Schuyler and I would sit in my office and discuss the deeper issues of scripture and how we might apply them to our lives. I could see, very clearly, that Schuyler wanted to make an impact upon the world and more importantly, leave an abiding legacy for generations. That being said, it was little surprise when I was asked to write a forward to a book written by this inspiring young man. One remarkable aspect of meeting and knowing someone when they are in the valley of decision or struggling to find their way, is that when they are on the mountaintop of success you can say, I knew them when. I do not believe you could meet a more authentic, reflective and self-assessing person.

When I was attending Christ for the Nations Bible College at King's Cathedral and Chapels, in Kahului, Maui, I had to read a book called "The Practice of the Presence of God," written by Brother Lawrence. His Monastic Brotherhood in Paris, where Brother Lawrence labored as a humble cook and dishwasher, for his Abbot, first published the book in 1693. The premise of the book was that we could live in unbroken communion with God, no matter what our duty or vocation was. Brother Lawrence found that he could meet with God and continually commune with God, just as much as when he was doing his sacerdotal duties, as he could while he was cooking or doing dishes. This was an extraordinary revelation in the 1600's, much like Martin Luther's revelation of Ephesians 2:8-9, "For by grace you have been saved through faith. And this is not your own doing; it is the gift of God, not a result of works, so that no one may boast" (ESV). Martin Luther posted his "Ninety-five

Theses" on the church door at Wittenberg, Germany in 1517, which eventually helped lead a movement to establish a counter-cultural revolution against the Catholic Church. I have no way to know if "Finding Jesus in the Dish Room" will become such a timeless classic as "The Practice of the Presence of God," but it certainly has all the makings of an enduring masterpiece.

My prayer as you read "Finding Jesus in the Dish Room" is that, like Brother Lawrence, you are drawn into a renewed hope, honestly assessing your filtration mechanism's for channeling the presence of God throughout the climate of your home, church, job, parish, synagogue, or even your own dish room. My parents, Bob and Kaye Gannon had a saying, "Bloom where you are planted." May God bloom in the dish rooms of your life as you become an exhibit for the power and presence of God. Schuyler Vowell has begun the conversation in "Finding Jesus in the Dish Room," now let's bring the conversation to the world around about us.

Enjoy reading,

Dr. Michael Walsh Gannon, Ph.D., L.C.A.D.C., BCPCC
President of Glass Ceiling Christian Counseling
www.glassceilingchristiancounseling.com

Introduction

I am twenty years old, I recently dropped out of Bible College, I currently have $15.26 in my checking account, and my girlfriend dumped me. Oh, and I'm a pastor. Because I am a Christian, I think I am better than you. I've never drank a beer, never smoked the devil's lettuce, and I look down on everyone who does. I judge you. I think you're going to burn in hell for watching R-rated movies and listening to rap music. Don't even get me started on tattoos. I don't cuss, I think sex is just a necessary evil; I don't think impure thoughts, or look at girls' butts. To sum it up, I think I am perfect.

I was a young believer, washing dishes in a bar, when I first came across these hilarious stereotypes that people associated with being a Christian. Some are true. Shockingly enough, most aren't. *Gasp*. But in today's culture, these are the thoughts that come to mind when we hear the world Christian. We associate this word with bigotry, hate, and judgement. None of these reflect what it truly means to be a Christian. To truly be a Christian means to follow Jesus. Christianity is not about all the "thou shalt nots." Christianity at its center is being a shining light for the Gospel. Our culture's perspective has been blurred. Misconceptions are seen as facts, lies considered truths. The misconceptions are endless. Growing up, I thought of God as this austere Santa Claus sitting in the sky on a huge golden throne, holding a lightning bolt, ready to sling it at me when I screwed up. I screwed up a lot and, come to think of it, I've never been struck by lightning. So either God throws like Jay Cutler and his throws sail over my head where they are intercepted and returned for six points, *or* he's not throwing any lightning at all. Lord knows I deserved a few bolts but that's not how Jesus rolls. That's not his style. It was in the dish room that I truly found Jesus. I found him behind blind misconceptions; I found him behind my self-inflicted pain; I found him with his arms open wide ready to embrace my sinful life. I saw others turn away from him because they were unable to see past the stereotypes, to get past their pain, and to believe Jesus wanted their sin-dead lives. Some may call this a Christian book, and I wouldn't argue with that, but you don't have to believe what I do to keep reading. This book is a book about overcoming misconceptions, finding Jesus, and dealing with the emotional and spiritual pains this world of ours has to offer.

As I previously mentioned, I am a twenty-year-old Bible College dropout. So it goes without saying that I am no theologian. Heck, I'm not an author. I barely passed English in high school and almost was kicked off the newspaper staff my junior year. This right here is gospel for the ne'er do well, the addict, the chronic relapser, the hypocrite, the cheater, the unbeliever, and the lifelong Christian. This is gospel of real life. This is real life.

Without going into too much detail yet, let's just say this book began to take shape as a diary of sorts after I did something bad. In my mind, I did something that caused me to fall from grace and I really began to sit back and question my faith. Not question *the* faith, but question my own. When everything was gone, how strong was my foundation? I used to wash dishes and try to give all the people I worked with advice as any good little Christian would do, but then I found myself in a situation where I had to practice what I preached. I began to write this book to myself. So if you get insulted by something I say, don't take it personally. Writing out and seeing what God's word says helped me, and I believe it will help you whether you're reading this at home or in a prison cell. Jesus once said, "In this life, you will encounter seasons that suck, but take heart, I overcame the world" (I might've slightly paraphrased that). Difficult seasons will come, but take heart.

This world I find myself in looks bleak. It looks scary. It's so uncertain that I'm second guessing most of the decisions I've made in my life leading up to this moment. I find myself more frequently asking, "Did I hear his voice correctly? Did he have this planned all along? Did I make this happen? Did I wander off the path he laid for me? Is this a test?" This is that pivotal moment in my life. I thought it had come before. I thought it was another time. But no, this is that one pivotal moment we all get. Our world falls apart. Then comes conviction. Then we reflect. Now we act. But this last stage is the moment that will define us. This moment is the moment that people will recall when we're talked about in small circles. Or large groups. Or when they write about us in history books. This is the moment people will remember when we're long gone. This is the moment where we actually get to choose. We've lost everything. And when the final verdict was made, it was out of our hands. We had no choice. But this right here, in this moment, you can choose your next step. Life or death. Wallow in self-pity or make the choice to live. Live without guilt, shame, disappointment. But with this choice comes a realization. We are powerless. How ironic? The one choice we have left, and our best option, is to realize we have no real power to change our situation at all. But there is freedom in surrendering to Jesus. The beauty of this surrender is that it doesn't mean you failed, it means you are on your way to real victory. It means you are on your way to true life.

Though when I think about my mistakes, I feel like I'm dying, little by little, day by day. It has nothing to do with nature or my growing older. My dying is of my own doing; I'm the cause of my own destruction. We are the pitfalls that ail society. We caused the black holes in our hearts. We look for love not knowing what it really is. Infatuation with the idea and concept of it but with no real grasp of the implications our actions may lead us to. We sacrifice real love for moments of pleasure. We sacrifice real moments for moments that don't last. We live for now, with reckless abandon because that's what society teaches. Just do it. Chase the wind and maybe you'll find yourself. Maybe I'll give Buddhism a chance, Christians are such hypocrites. Chase whatever satisfies your appetite, even if it's just for a moment. Live and love by the feelings you currently have. Live and love by the standard of this world. Live and love at the expense of the people who care about you. Live and love with selfishness. Do what makes you happy. That's the message we hear and tend to model our lives after. As the street poet Drake once said, "You only live once." So enjoy every second. Is our life meant to be like this? One big mess of love and heartbreak and happiness and pain? Are we doing this life thing right? Are we being warped by our culture? Are we being tainted? Is our generation being corrupted? Is there room for religion? We're dying inside. Little by little. Everyday. And it's our own doing. We have mastered the art of losing everything.

I'm writing this sitting on my toilet. It's four o'clock in the afternoon and the first time I've managed to slide out of my bed today. I'd honestly like to crawl in a hole and let someone bury me. I've done a lot of wrong in my life but this may take the cake. I should be living to a higher standard. I mean, I'm not only a Christian, I was just ordained. I shouldn't be giving into temptation. I shouldn't let the world get me down. God is good, all the time. All the time, God is good. Feel free to add in your own Christian cliché. Shouldn't I, of all people, know that God is good? Shouldn't my strength be renewed knowing this fact? Shouldn't I be soaring on wings like eagles? Shouldn't I walk and not grow weary? Shouldn't pain just bounce off me because I know Jesus already bore it on the cross? Shouldn't this hole in my heart be mended because Jesus told me to "take heart?" For he has already overcome the world. I have no doubt that God is good. I know his throne is not in jeopardy. He's doing just fine. But I'm not. And that's okay. I honestly don't even have the strength to leave my bathroom. My eyes hurt. My face is raw. My stomach is in knots. My body feels numb. I just stare at my reflection in the mirror and I notice my hair is an unkept shaggy mop and my skimpy beard is just a mess of uneven stubble. I don't smell particularly good either. Although I look terrible, I feel worse.

I have to remind myself that this isn't a bad dream. This isn't a nightmare. This isn't just in my head. God, I wish it was. I wish I would wake up and this would all be in my head. I'd wake up and find this isn't really happening. But this is reality. I can't blame this on anyone. I wish I could. That might make me feel better. Probably not. I screwed up. And this was my last chance. Third chance actually. Three strikes, I'm out. There's no sense arguing over the call. The umpire is absolutely justified in the reason for the call. I didn't even swing. I just watched the ball go by me and turned toward the dugout. Maybe nobody saw. Nope, here come the hecklers. Blowing up my Twitter feed. Here come the naysayers. Only now they are vindicated. I screwed up like they said I would. No sense begging. This is how it has to be. When you're at your lowest, the only way is up.

So my first step is to get off this toilet. Take a shower. Brush my teeth. Do something with this mop on my head. Shave this peach fuzz off my face. Well maybe not, it's taken me a month to get this. I may just ride it out.

At this point you're probably wondering what I did. You're probably wondering what my story is. Why I'm sitting on a toilet at four in the afternoon after a sleepless night of replaying images in my head and wondering to yourself what any of this has to do with Jesus. You may be wondering what I did. And I'm not going to tell you. Why? Because I know you know this feeling. I know you've been where I am, and if you haven't, I pray to God you never are, but it is likely you too will metaphorically (or perhaps literally) be on your toilet at four in the afternoon, feeling hopeless. It's a sad reality that we will all face this moment in our lives. We will all feel this pain. We will all feel this disappointment. We will all feel that we are dying inside. We will all be here, and often it's our own doing. We will all have our own four in the afternoon. I did what you did; screwed up. It's not important what, but you and I are in the same boat. But thank God, Jesus didn't come for perfect people. He came for people that messed up.

CHAPTER ONE

So Who is Jesus?

"God in the flesh?"
"Son of God?"
"Deliverer?"
"Savior?"
"Nobody?"
"Heavenly father?"
"Good teacher of morality?"
"Liar?"
"Deceiver?"
"Who is Jesus?" I asked these questions to a lot of people and it just seemed to make everyone uncomfortable. I asked a friend of mine who happens to be a pastor and his response was, "That's a loaded question." I texted this question to a friend of mine in Florida who has no religious affiliation and he didn't text back and I still haven't heard from him. And if you're reading this, you missed out on a chance to be in a book. Some

people just shrugged and said things like, "Nobody to me, personally," or, "I'm not sure," or, "He's a crutch for people who can't handle life on their own." However, there were people who couldn't wait to proclaim all the amazing things Jesus has done for them and give me answers like, "The love of my life," and, "For reasons I'll never understand, he saved me and set me free." So who is this Jesus guy? How can he be everything to some people and nothing to others? Is he who he claims to be? Who does he claim to be? Was he even a real person?

Upon having conversations with many unbelievers, satanists, atheists, agnostics; in fairness, I can't say this about all of them but for the vast majority, Jesus seems to be the epitome of all the things they hate about religion. They hate church, they hate church people, and they hate being told what to do. They don't like accountability so they dismiss the idea of God so they can live in their sin and not feel convicted. They like their sin, so do not tell them that it is wrong, because that just makes you a hater. Haters gonna hate, hate, hate and we all know Christians are the ultimate haters and hypocrites. Christians are hypocrites because we sin and hide behind our religion when we can't cope with the real world, and then we stand behind Jesus and point our judgmental finger at everybody else because we're perfect and everyone else is going to hell. We conceive this notion of being born again because we hate ourselves and the only way to feel better about our terrible lives is to become, "someone new." Religion sucks.

I agree with that last part. I am not religious. Jesus was not religious. What if I told you Jesus came to abolish religion? Would that shock you?

Jesus came at a time when religion was rampant. Jesus sought to teach us how to go from religion to relationship. Religion says, "do" and Jesus said, "done." Religion is about "thou shalt not." Jesus is about grace and love. Religion is unforgiving; it's about constantly striving to become worthy of salvation. A relationship is about walking with God. Jesus knows we aren't going to be good enough for salvation and he forgives us anyway. He knew most of the world would never love him but he died for them anyway. Christians aren't perfect. We don't claim to be. We are all sinners, and we understand that. That is why we desperately need a savior. We're as broken as the world and that is why we cling to Jesus, why we go to church, and why we worship him. Because even when we're at our worst, he loves us unconditionally. When we accept Jesus into our lives, the old life is gone and we become a new creation. This isn't because we cannot cope with the real world, it is because we are sick and tired of living in our sin, and Jesus is so gracious he cleanses us and makes us new.

I love the Bible. The Bible is a divinely inspired book that shows all of us how we fit in this world contrary to what people may believe, it is not a rule book, it is a love story. I believe that everything written in it is divinely inspired by God and he used normal guys to write it. If you do not believe that, that is alright with me, so I hope it's alright with you that I do. Nobody has all the answers, including myself, but I hope you continue reading with an open mind. The Bible was written for real people facing real issues and is the antidote for our problems. It also tells us who Jesus is. It is widely accepted that Jesus was, in fact, a real person that walked the earth about two thousand years ago. Most major religions accept that he was a good prophet, or a good teacher of morality and nothing more than that but the Bible claims he is a lot more. Let's stop there for a second. If Jesus claimed to be God, which he did, and it turned out he wasn't, then that would make Jesus a liar. Therefore, he would not be a good teacher of morals at all if he's constantly lying. So he can't just be a good teacher of morals and nothing more. He's either who he claims to be or he's nuts. So who did he claim to be? In Jesus's own words, he says in John 8:58, "'Believe me'," said Jesus, '*I am who I am* long before Abraham was anything.'" Jesus referring to himself as "I am" is a clear reference to Exodus 3:14 (MSG) where God calls himself "I am." Also a couple chapters later in John 10:30 Jesus says, "I and the Father are one heart and mind." (MSG). He is definitely making a claim that he is God in the flesh.

So who cares? Why does it matter to me if he was or wasn't what he claimed to be? Because if he was not God, but only a crazy hippie with long hair and sandals skipping around telling confusing stories and doing magic tricks, then obviously his death would have been meaningless and by that I mean his death would not have been sufficient to pay the penalty for our sins.

You see, before Jesus was on the earth, there was a divide between us and God because he could not look upon sin, but along came Jesus as the ultimate sacrifice. He was the bridge we needed to get to God. He was God in the flesh and he came and lived a sinless life and performed miracles and acts of love and compassion. He showed us how to live. He was crucified and died in our place, a death only we deserved so we wouldn't have to, and on his cross, he bore all our sin, all our guilt, our shame, our worries, our fears and his last three words here send chills down the devil's spine, "It is finished." Three days later, he rose from the grave, having conquered death and sin. It is finished. At that moment, sin lost its power; death lost its sting.

Only God has the power to pay such a debt. Jesus had to be God in order to have the authority to pay for our sins, but he also had to be man so he could die. Salvation comes through faith in Jesus Christ and why he professed in John 14:6, "I am the way and the truth and the life. No one comes to the Father except through me." (ESV).

In this statement, he not only claims to be the only way to salvation, he claims to be the truth. He is truth. He is life. He, as the incarnate word of God, is the epitome of absolute truth. He's not a liar. He is the source of life. Jesus claimed he would lay down his life for his sheep (us) and then take it back up again. He had authority over death. He broke the chains of sin and death off of our lives so that we could live, and live more abundantly.

―― CHAPTER TWO ――

God the Father?

Throughout this book called the Bible, the authors liken this vast deity, this creator of the universe, this omnipotent, omnipresent God to a father. Father isn't a common term in the Old Testament when referring to God, but we see in the New Testament Jesus teaching the disciples to address and pray to God as Abba or Father. When I was a child, I remember my father smelled of rubbing alcohol and tobacco. He wore a flannel shirt, a dirty ball cap, and a frown the majority of the time. He was slightly overweight, his head was bald, and he loved to yell. My parents split up when I was young and after a custody battle, the courts decided I could visit my father every other weekend. I remember being so excited to see him and visit. I longed to spend more time with him. I wanted to know him better. And every time I would get to his house for our two days together, he would buy me McDonald's Happy Meals and take me to Wal-Mart and let me get whatever toy I wanted. I would sit in the floorboard of his tractor and sleep while he plowed the ground for hours. We would throw baseball in the backyard and watch the Yankees play. But as is normal for little kids, my sisters and I would play too loud, make too much noise, and make messes we were incapable of cleaning up. Then we would see the side of my father we all hated. His eyes would squint, his face would become red with anger, and he would spit as he cussed at us and called us stupid. As a kid, the hardest thing in the world to take was to see the man I admired most calling me stupid for messing up. There was always this longing to prove myself to him. I felt the need to earn the Happy Meal and action figure he gave me. I walked on eggshells around him but I would have walked on glass shards barefoot if it would make him proud of me.

Growing up, I heard God was my father so I assumed God washed his face with wintergreen rubbing alcohol, wore a Yankees hat, flannel shirts that reeked of tobacco warehouses, and smoked cigarillos. I pictured God as the man I was allowed to visit for a few hours on Sunday morning. I wanted to please him but it seemed impossible. I wanted him to be proud of me but the more I tried, the more I messed up. As I grew up, I wasn't knocking my small cup full of Hi-C onto the McDonald's floor, but the older I got, the more serious my screw ups were and in my head, I pictured God squinting his eyes, his face becoming red with anger, and he would spit as he cussed at me and called me stupid.

Into my teenage years, the relationship between my father and I was the worst it had ever been. We couldn't talk without fighting. We hated each other. There was nothing I could do or say that would make him proud to be my father. From age thirteen to eighteen, I could probably count the times my father smiled on one hand. As our relationship grew more strenuous, so did my relationship with my Heavenly Father. Frankly, the thought of God as my father was frightening. My dad would fly off the handle at the littlest things and this God has all these rules that I break everyday so he must really be pissed at me. So I just assumed he was in Heaven cussing me out, calling me stupid, and there was nothing I could possibly do to earn a Happy Meal and an action figure from him. I didn't want God to be my father. I didn't want him to be my anything. The idea of God as my father, to me personally, only represented another father figure I would disappoint, anger, and let down. It was better to just dislike him just like I disliked my father.

I talk to a lot of people and they have a similar view of God. He may not smell like tobacco and wear a Yankees hat but he represents their own version of an angry old man. So how do we settle this problem? For me, I had to learn what God really thought of me. I had to figure out how my Heavenly Father viewed me. It is revealed to us in the Bible how he sees his children and it is evident through scripture that God is not waving his arm in the air and yelling at you to get off his lawn. God loved us so much he was willing to leave the comfort of Heaven, take on flesh and bone, enter humanity in the incarnation of Jesus, in order to live a sinless perfect life, and then be brutally murdered. For you. Yes, you read that right. For you. The God of the universe died for you and also for people who would never reciprocate the same love. He knew we could never pay him back. He doesn't ask or expect us to because we weren't saved because we were good, we were saved because of how good God is and how much God loves us. He freely gives you that Happy Meal. We are so freely given gifts that we could never begin to repay just because God loves us. He doesn't wear a scowl; he wears a smile. He doesn't yell when you spill your Hi-C, and he doesn't call you names. He is a Yankees fan though.

— CHAPTER THREE —

No Way, Hosea

Since Jesus is God in the flesh, to better understand Jesus would be to better understand God and his love for us. I felt it was fitting to focus this chapter around probably one of the most well-known verses in the Bible, the verse Tim Tebow wrote—John 3:16. Although it is so well-known, I want to take another look at this verse in a way that allows us to truly understand it. "For God so loved the world, he gave his only begotten son that whosoever believes in him will have eternal life."

    I've been to concerts and seen teenage girls lined up outside of a tour bus absolutely losing their mind at just the sight of a rock star or famous personality. Years ago when we were younger, my older sister was obsessed with a certain boy band. It was unhealthy. She knew everything about them. She knew where they came from, what their birthdays were, how many hairs were on their head, and what they ate for breakfast in the mornings. She had posters of them up all over her room. She was such a huge fan she started dressing like them and would buy magazines if they even mentioned this band. She knew all their songs by heart and learned the guitar so she could play their songs. She so loved them. I felt it was my responsibility as her younger brother to tell her how weird her obsession was. I mean, how crazy is it to be absolutely obsessed with and love somebody that probably, more than likely, will never even know you exist and will never reciprocate the love you have for them? That's just crazy. Why would you put so much effort into knowing about them and knowing them and loving someone who won't ever love you back? See where I'm going with this?

Yes, I just compared God to a teenage fangirl. God is your biggest fan. He loves you. He doesn't just love you, he *so* loves you. He has your poster up in his room. The Bible says he even knows the hairs on your head. This is mind-boggling to me. I want to pull God aside and be like, "God, c'mon, man. This isn't healthy. Do you realize you love people, not only that, you died for people who will never know you?" If you look at the verse, it says, God so loved the world. The word "world" here is referencing the sinful culture and society absent of God. He sent his son to die for these people. The bad people. Not just the good people, the noble people, or the upstanding people. Jesus didn't die just for the people who would reciprocate his love or just for the people who would acknowledge him. He sent his son for everybody. God had so much love and compassion for you that he sent his son to die, with no guarantees from us, and with just the chance that you might love and accept him.

So let me get this straight. God loved us so much, he came down here, took on flesh and bones, died in our place, at the chance, perhaps, possibly, we might accept his sacrifice and what he has done for us and he did all of this with no strings attached? Yes. He is obsessed with you, he knows all about you, every nook and cranny of your heart, and what you ate for breakfast this morning. He answered the question of if he cares, and if he is involved in humanity. He did so in the form of Jesus Christ who was born into this humanity to save it. He showed he does care, so much so, he was willing to die for you and for me.

There is a story in the Old Testament that paints a vivid picture of the crazy, irrational, fangirl-love God has for us. In the book of Hosea, there is a story of a guy named, well, Hosea. But Hosea was not just any guy, he was a prophet of God. He was the man who spoke on God's behalf about his plans and his love. He was one of the most well-known people in all of Israel. When he walked in the room, people acknowledged him and gave him high fives. He was the big man on campus. Hosea also got one of the weirdest assignments by God.

The prophets of the Old Testament all exemplified behavior that by today's standards would have had them institutionalized. Such as wandering around naked and once shaving his beard with a sword. But back to what I was saying, Hosea got a pretty rough assignment, and me personally, I would have rather walked around the desert naked and shaved my beard with a sword, than marry a prostitute like Hosea was commanded. Imagine that conversation.

"Hosea."

"Hey, what's up, God?"

"I want you to get married."

"Oh, okay, that's great. I'm sure you've picked out a beautiful, wholesome woman for…"

"I want you to marry a hooker."

"LOL."

"Her name is Gomer."

"Oh. You're serious? I mean, I'm a pastor. I'm a man of God. I can't marry a hooker."

"You're going to marry her and have three kids together."

So Hosea obeyed God and went to the red light district and found his bride, the prostitute, Gomer. They get married and the Bible says they have kids together so things were probably going pretty well. One day, Hosea wakes up and his wife, Gomer, has left him and their kids. Overnight, he has become a single dad. Time goes by and God speaks to Hosea again telling him to go find his wife who has left, turned her back on her family, and gone back to prostituting.

Imagine the anguish Hosea felt as he, the prophet of God, wanders back through the dark, back alleys of the red light district looking for his adulterous wife. Imagine the looks, imagine the laughs, and imagine the tweets. "OMG, just saw my pastor at the brothel." The situation got even worse when he finds her. He not only finds her but he has to pay for her. Keep in mind, she is his wife, she is already his and he has to purchase her. Imagine her shame when she saw Hosea coming. Imagine how shocked she was when he bought her. She knew she was undeserving, she left him after all. We know he roughly spent a year's worth of wages purchasing his wife back. I think you and I would agree she wasn't worth that much. But he came back for her, even though she didn't deserve it.

Later on, God reveals that this is a portrayal of his love for us. I'm Gomer. You're Gomer. I want to be good, and I try to be good, but too often I find myself where I shouldn't be, doing things I shouldn't be doing, wrapped up in old sin. But my Hosea will always come back for me. You and I belong to God, he created us. We are his, yet he willingly paid a costly price for us. He paid the price not in shekels but he paid the price of his own life in the form of his son Jesus Christ. The Bible says he already knows who will receive him, yet he desires that everyone be saved. He did not just die for those who would love him back. He was beaten, tortured, and crucified because he loved people who would never love him back, and he knew that. He died for people who would never choose him. The extent of this kind of love is irrational. It makes absolutely no sense. This love is ours. Is it too good to be true? No way, Hosea.

―― CHAPTER FOUR ――

Listen to your Heart?

Listen to your heart. Follow your heart. We've all heard this saying. It's sung about in songs, it's portrayed in movies, and it's often the theme of our own lives. "Listen to your heart," is just a nice, accepted way of saying, do what you want or do what you desire. The Bible says, and I believe few would argue, the heart is wicked. Yes, of course, hearts can be compassionate and loving, but they often want one thing and then want something completely different the very next day. Hearts are emotional, and emotions can go in every direction. And our desires aren't always good. My desires aren't always good. I don't know about you, but that scares me sometimes.

When I was younger, because I'm so grown up now, I struggled with following my heart. Which, as a sixteen-year-old kid, meant I want this girl today and I want this girl tomorrow, and ultimately, I did not care about hurting anybody's feelings because, after all, I was only doing what my heart wants. After I got saved a few months prior to my eighteenth birthday, I assumed since I was saved and received Christ, that I would be rid of all these carnal thoughts and desires. All my bad thoughts would be gone. Just like that. I would no longer struggle with dirty thoughts or lust. Well that turned out not to be the case. We all struggle with desires that aren't so Christian. We always will.

Since I've been saved, I've done un-Christianly things. But as a sixteen year old kid, texting three girls at once isn't a huge deal, but as a twenty-year-old, who is a pastor and church planter, now leading a campus ministry, texting multiple girls while in a committed relationship would be a big deal. But that doesn't mean the desire isn't there. I know God has called me, and sometimes I want to give up because too often, those thoughts creep in my head that remind me of those ungodly desires and that ultimately I will give in and the higher I get is only a setup for how far I will fall.

Desires seek to tell you that they are, in fact, you. They want you to begin to believe that they are your real nature. Desires seek to tell you that they are not just impulses or appetites, they are perpetual desires you genuinely crave, and constitute who you really are. And they're strong. Desires want you to yield to them and succumb to them and they want to define your course. Desires tell you not to resist, because what you feel is completely normal, it's completely natural. C'mon man just follow your heart.

I don't want to follow my heart because I do not trust it. My heart is fickle, and my emotions are all over the place. Often times, the desires of my heart feel like they're trapping me and holding me back. Why would I want to follow the very thing wanting to build me up ultimately so I have farther to fall?

I sometimes desire to lie, cheat, deceive, or take the easy way out and I think to myself and talk to God and honestly say, "God, I feel like I shouldn't still be in this place spiritually." Meaning, I feel like I should be past this. I don't want to speak for everyone, but I'm sure you often feel that way.

"Lord, I'm reading my Bible every day and praying but I still feel these desires pulling me in a negative direction."

"Jesus, I'm pastoring and leading. Why am I still struggling with this?"

The prophet Jeremiah even poses the question regarding the heart, "Who can understand it?"

The Bible challenges us to not follow the heart but question it. So ask yourself why do I want this, and where would giving into this particular desire take me? From the heart comes jealousy and from the heart comes adultery. These desires are of this world and often a result of accepting ideas and notions of it. The "world" can roughly be defined as ideology and culture absent from God. I am as guilty as anyone of accepting and eating up this world. And ultimately, that has affected my desires and my appetite. It has affected my thought process as well as life circumstances, my priorities, and, sadly, my morals. The Bible says to not be of the world but that process doesn't happen overnight. The principles and values not found in the Bible are everywhere around you vying for your attention. But these will never satisfy you, they will never fulfill you, and they will leave you desiring more. You will find yourself digging yourself out of a deep hole.

The disciple John writes numerous times in 1 John the phrase "overcome the world." To me, this means "overpower your desires." How do you overpower desires and ideas that are absent from God that will leave you completely unsatisfied? He tells us that those who believe and have faith in Jesus can overcome the world. Through our faith in Jesus, and that alone, is the key to defeating and overpowering desires of this world.

So if there is so much power there, why do I still want to text other girls? Why do I turn the treadmill up a few levels at the gym when a blonde girl in yoga pants gets on the one next to me? John says overcoming comes from faith and a belief in Jesus. Well, I believe and I still want to run on the treadmill a few extra minutes because of the girl in tight pants next to me.

Do we really know what belief is? I had the revelation that maybe I didn't quite understand what kind of belief John is talking about. He's talking about a lifestyle. He's talking about a relationship. And every time we reach out to God, we overpower. We overcome. Desires outside of God are hollow and fruitless and will never lead you where God can. Those who immerse themselves in Jesus and his goodness and his beauty and in a relationship with the living God are the overcomers. When we accepted Jesus, we were born again. We became spiritually new creations. There's something birthed inside you and momentum has started to build, momentum that Jesus intends to use to get you to where he wants you. These desires will often try to stop the momentum and stop your forward progress and get between you and Jesus. Realize the power that is already in you and building inside of you. God has already taken hold of you. You are more than the desires. Don't underestimate what he has already done inside of you and in your life. There is a God and I want to know him and live for him, and I want to spend eternity with him. I want him to be the most real thing in my life.

─── CHAPTER FIVE ───

Does God Have a Plan for Me?

When God is not the center of our lives, we get caught in this monotonous cycle of trying to better ourselves, accomplish more, and be more (But if you're like my friend, you're a seventh-year senior, frying foods, and wondering, "What am I doing with my life?"). Naturally, we have ambition and want a great job, to find a great girl or guy to marry, get a nice house, and of course, drive a new car. And there's nothing wrong with that. But then reality hits, and you find yourself digging in your cup holder for nickels so you can buy a McDouble. Not exactly living the dream.

One night when the dinner rush was over and the kitchen was clean, my coworker and I hid in the back of the kitchen away from the noisy bar crowd. The conversation started off as it typically would, with complaints about school and working too many hours, but things took a turn when he began to talk about his struggle to find his place and purpose in this life. He wasn't sure what he was supposed to be doing. I've often found myself feeling the same way. I feel like we've all been here. We're just not quite sure if we're in God's plan. Or if he even has one for us. My friend told me life wasn't working out the way he wanted and he just couldn't believe that Jesus died with him in mind and the idea that this Jesus guy would even care what happens to him, nevertheless actually have a plan for his life, it was just too hard to believe. So the question is, does God have a plan for your life? Does he care? Yes. Even if it doesn't feel like it, he does. If we turn to the scriptures, we see in Ephesians 2:10 that, "He creates each of us by Christ Jesus to join him in the work he does, the good work he has gotten ready for us to do, work we had better be doing." This shows he not only created you but created you with a purpose and a plan for you to fulfill.

Well what about someone who isn't actively pursuing a relationship with Jesus, like my friend? Jesus decides to answer a similar question with three stories. Classic Jesus. The religious people of the day, the Pharisees, asked Jesus why he hung out with people with notorious reputations. In other words, why do you associate with people who aren't actively pursuing a relationship with God? His response is found in the book of John. Does a shepherd care about sheep that wandered off? What about a rebellious son, does his father still love him and plan for his return? We see in scripture where Jesus answers these questions, as well as a lot more. In the story Jesus told regarding the lost sheep, he explains that a shepherd owns one hundred sheep and one of the hundred wanders off, and gets lost. This shepherd doesn't say, "Well it's just one sheep." No, he leaves the ninety-nine to save the one. Unlike the sheep, the son in the next story wasn't oblivious in his wandering. He knowingly turned his back on his father and left with his inheritance. The son demands his inheritance and then leaves home in pursuit of a good time, in pursuit of what he thought would make his life better. But eventually, he was a seventh-year senior frying foods, metaphorically speaking, wondering, "What the heck am I doing?"

Things were not going well. He had lost his money and his dignity as well. He returns home to his father and requests to just be a servant, not feeling worthy of being a son anymore. I mean, why would he? He disgraced his father, left, and lived sinfully. So, did his father say, "Go feed the pigs!" No! He welcomed him like a king and threw a party in his honor!

Now with all that in mind, the shepherd may tend to keep a more watchful eye on this particular sheep and perhaps the same could be said for the father and son. But if anything, this would not be showing a lack of love, quite the opposite actually. God loves you enough to help you even if you may not like it. He may give you guidance you do not like, but it is guidance nonetheless. I heard all through my years of sports that it was a bad sign if your coach stopped coaching you. That meant he had washed his hands of you. It would be a waste of breath to give you advice or correction. The Lord, however, will continue to coach you and guide you as long as you let him. Romans 8:28 says, "That's why we can be so sure that every detail in our lives of love for God is worked into something good." (ESV). This means that God will work out all things for the good of those who love him.

The belief that Jesus has a plan for your life has to start with a trust in him. A trust in his timing, and a trust in his fairness. He has a plan for you but it may not be the plan we have for ourselves and we have to learn to set aside our desires and plans and trust in him that we what we get is what he wants us to have. Ultimately, trusting in Jesus and his plan is trusting in his will for our lives. And it's easy to get sucked into the monotonous striving of worldly status or material wealth, such as money and cars. It's even easier to look at what so-and-so has and begin to think about how unfair life is and how unfair God is. If we let the world dictate our feeling of success, then that's what we're left with. Feeling like we came up short, that we're not fulfilling our potential because when we look over the fence and our neighbor has just a little bit more than we do. So it's easy to feel inadequate or that we deserve more compared to someone else. Jesus said in Matthew 20 one of the most frustrating things he ever said, in my opinion. He said, "Many of the first ending up last, and the last first." Jesus is basically telling us the people you counted out are my number ones and your number ones aren't in my top twenty-five. The parable Jesus teaches is so frustrating to me because I have often found myself striving and trying to fit into the world's ranking system.

Matthew 20:1-16 says, "God's kingdom is like an estate manager who went out early in the morning to hire workers for his vineyard. They agreed on a wage of a dollar a day, and went to work.

Later, about nine o'clock, the manager saw some other men hanging around the town square unemployed. He told them to go to work in his vineyard and he would pay them a fair wage. They went.

He did the same thing at noon, and again at three o'clock. At five o'clock, he went back and found still others standing around. He said, 'Why are you standing around all day doing nothing?'

They said, 'Because no one hired us.'

He told them to go to work in his vineyard.

When the day's work was over, the owner of the vineyard instructed his foreman, 'Call the workers in and pay them their wages. Start with the last hired and go on to the first.'

Those hired at five o'clock came up and were each given a dollar. When those who were hired first saw that, they assumed they would get far more. But they got the same, each of them one dollar. Taking the dollar, they groused angrily to the manager, 'These last workers put in only one easy hour, and you just made them equal to us, who slaved all day under a scorching sun.'

He replied to the one speaking for the rest, 'Friend, I haven't been unfair. We agreed on the wage of a dollar, didn't we? So take it and go. I decided to give to the one who came last the same as you. Can't I do what I want with my own money? Are you going to get stingy because I am generous? Here it is again, the Great Reversal: many of the first ending up last, and the last first.'" (MSG).

To sum it up, the guys who worked twelve hours got paid the same as the guys who worked one hour and the crew that worked twelve hours wasn't particularly happy about it.

"Wait up! Hold on! Not fair! We worked all day in the sun and these guys only worked one hour! Dude, they still smell good for Pete's sake. They get the same as us? Where is the fairness in that?"

They have a valid complaint right? What's even more frustrating is that this is an illustration of how God's kingdom works. So what is Jesus saying here? God doesn't necessarily give us what we think we deserve. He gives us what he wants to give us and asks us to trust him that that is enough. If you're like I use to be you're thinking, "Well, hold on, I want to get what I deserve and I want to deserve what I get. If I work twelve hours, then I want to be paid more than the guy who only worked for one hour." That's a dead-end way of thinking and here's why.

How many of you have sinned? According to the Bible, the penalty for sin is death. Do you still want what you deserve? So let's stop worrying about what we "deserve" because if that played out, it wouldn't be pretty. You and I are products of grace. I heard something once and it has always stuck with me; "If Jesus never did another thing for us, he's already done more than we deserve."

In the parable, the first group was under a contract, but the last group was under grace. I would much rather live in the ambiguity of God's grace and fairness than in the world's measures of success.

It all comes down to this, do we trust Jesus? Do we trust that he's fair? Let God be God and even when you're a seventh-year senior frying foods, maintain your faith and trust he has a plan.

We are the eleventh-hour workers. We barely got in. When we met God, our lives were going nowhere.

God asked, "What are you doing here?"

We replied, "Not really sure. Nobody hired us."

God said, "I'll take you. You'll be mine. Follow me and I'll give you what is right."

The metaphor of working in the fields isn't to illustrate how difficult and labor-intensive it is to follow Jesus, it's to show us his generosity and how he pours out his grace and how he blesses us beyond what we think we deserve. Trust him. He knows us better than we know ourselves. He loves us more than we love ourselves. Let's not relate to God by a contract. Let God, in his infinite love, goodness, and fairness, give you what is right and you will receive exceedingly abundantly above all that you can ask, think, or even imagine. Trust him that he has a plan and trust that you have what is right in this season of your life.

CHAPTER SIX

Even If You Sleep with Your General's Wife, Get Her Pregnant, and then Have Him Killed, God Still Loves You

Thank God, our salvation isn't conditional in respect to our shortcomings. It is a free gift, given to us only by grace not because we are good, but because he is good. This revelation is not always enough to make your pain pack up and leave. It also doesn't make it any less true just because we may not feel like believing it. Just because I don't feel like trusting God has a plan for me, doesn't mean I should trust him any less. Sometimes we have to pick ourselves up and rub some dirt on it. It's hard, but we aren't the first people to screw up. Luckily, others were brave enough to record their own pain and suffering for us to see. One of these brave souls was King David, one of the mightiest men of God in all of history. God blessed him beyond his wildest dreams, from a lowly shepherd boy to a king. But he was only a man. Favored by God, yes without a doubt, but he was just a man—a man with temptations, a man with desires that weren't always Godly, a man sometimes with clouded judgment, a man who gave into temptations who did his best to throw it all away. He was a man who, in his clouded judgment and his fleshly desire, committed adultery and murder. So, if you think you've done too much wrong for God to love you and use you, think again. No doubt he felt guilt, shame, and disappointment. He felt convicted. He without a doubt laid in bed and didn't get a wink of sleep. He without a doubt laid in bed until four in the afternoon and sat on his toilet and cried. He suffered his four in the afternoon like everybody else. But he responded by writing one of the most beautiful passages in the Bible, Psalm 51.

"Generous in love—God, give grace! Huge in mercy—wipe out my bad record. Scrub away my guilt, soak out my sins in your laundry. I know how bad I've been; my sins are staring me down. You're the One I've violated, and you've seen it all, seen the full extent of my evil. You have all the facts before you; whatever you decide about me is fair. I've been out of step with you for a long time, in the wrong since before I was born. What you're after is truth from the inside out. Enter me, then; conceive a new, true life. Soak me in your laundry and I'll come out clean, scrub me and I'll have a snow-white life. Tune me in to foot-tapping songs, set these once-broken bones to dancing. Don't look too close for blemishes, give me a clean bill of health. God, make a fresh start in me, shape a Genesis week from the chaos of my life. Don't throw me out with the trash, or fail to breathe holiness in me. Bring me back from gray exile, put a fresh wind in my sails! Give me a job teaching rebels your ways so the lost can find their way home. Commute my death sentence, God, my salvation God, and I'll sing anthems to your life-giving ways. Unbutton my lips, dear God; I'll let loose with your praise. Going through the motions doesn't please you, a flawless performance is nothing to you. I learned God-worship when my pride was shattered. Heart-shattered lives ready for love don't for a moment escape God's notice. Make Zion the place you delight in, repair Jerusalem's broken-down walls. Then you'll get real worship from us, acts of worship small and large, including all the bulls they can heave onto your altar!" (MSG).

The strength of this passage speaks for itself. The power behind these words is unparalleled. We know this feeling. We know this shame and guilt. And maybe you've fallen on your face and prayed something similar. Maybe you haven't. Maybe you should. But the fact of the matter is, we mess up. We're human. It's an unavoidable scenario that will happen. And that's okay. Our God knew that. And so did David. He messed up. And rather than running down to the bar and making the situation way worse like I've seen far too many people do, he fell on his knees and cried out to God. Instead of calling his homie up, the one with the connections, you know the one, and getting high, he fell on his knees in surrender. Instead of calling that girl, the one who's "always there for you," he realized there wasn't a person on Earth who could take this shame away.

"Generous in love—God, give grace! Huge in mercy—wipe out my bad record. Scrub away my guilt, soak out my sins in your laundry. I know how bad I've been; my sins are staring me down."

Pray that. Take a deep breath. Feel a little bit of that chip on your shoulder break off. God knows we don't deserve it. We've done so much wrong. We're broken sinners. But he loves us beyond imagine. It's unfathomable. It doesn't matter who you are, it doesn't matter if you have it all together or if you are a straight OG from the streets, we all have these two things in common:

1. The desire to be loved
2. The desire to love

As a result of this, our generation has this absolute obsession with the idea. We don't know what real love is yet, but the idea sounds so good. Love is just business in our society. Think about the music you listen to. Most songs revolve around the concept of love or heartbreak or trying to win someone's love. Most movies with a love story do really well. If you love someone, you will have to sit through a few romantic comedies, just a fact. Guys, you will have to at some point sit down and watch a Nicholas Sparks movie. That is unavoidable.

Our culture is so hungry for a love they just can't seem to find so they are accepting fakes. Duplicates. Counterfeits. This just shows how desperately our generation is searching for something real. But here's the big question: how can you know what love is, if you aren't aware of *who* love is?

Jesus is love. This love though is different than anything on this earth. This is not Christian-mingle love. This isn't normal-relationship love. This love breaks every stronghold, every chain; this love breathes life where there is death. This love turns a broken sinner into a blessing. This love forgives. This is the love we have been searching for.

The problem is that we, in our culture, haven't seemed to grasp that. We look for love in the bar, or the internet, or in that person whose number you knew you should've deleted a long time ago. We try to find it in things of this world and fill that void that's growing bigger day by day. We have to turn to the cross and realize the cross is love. We look for this love but will never find it until we have the revelation that it only comes when we cross that bridge which is the cross of Jesus Christ. People see the cross as a religious symbol, a cliché. They see hate, bigotry, hypocrisy, religion, oppression. No. You cannot get love without the cross. You cannot have the cross without the love. This love is extraordinary. This is healing. This is mending. This is reparation. Romans 8:38-39 puts it best, "I'm absolutely convinced that nothing—nothing living or dead, angelic or demonic, today or tomorrow, high or low, thinkable or unthinkable—absolutely nothing can get between us and God's love because of the way that Jesus our Master has embraced us." This means there is nothing so bad that you can do that would cause God to love you any less.

"You're the One I've violated, and you've seen it all, seen the full extent of my evil. You have all the facts before you; whatever you decide about me is fair.

I've been out of step with you for a long time, in the wrong since before I was born. What you're after is truth from the inside out. Enter me, then; conceive a new, true life."

There's no sense hiding it. He knows what you've done. Before you get embarrassed, He is not condemning you. He does however, as the scripture says, "have all the facts." And it follows that with, "whatever you decide about me is fair." This is not very reassuring. What I deserve is death. I don't deserve grace. I don't deserve mercy. I don't deserve his love. I knew what God had called me to do. I knew he called me to rise about the temptations of this world, to set myself apart. I knew this. And I gave in anyway. Just like David, "I've been out of step with you for a long time, in the wrong since before I was born." We all can relate to David here, feeling so out of step with God when we really sit back and assess the damage. We see that we've been out of sync with God for a while. We didn't even know it. But seeing the damage now, it is apparent we wandered off his path and down our own. But the Lord is after truth. Sincerity. Genuine repentance. "What you're after is truth from the inside out." Up to this point, we may have been lying to ourselves. We just wanted to give into temptation. It was so easy. It wouldn't cost us anything. Just go for it. That's what grace is for anyway, right? These are just lies and excuses we build up for our own selfish agenda. Let's just be honest. We sinned against God. We hurt a lot of people, including ourselves. With this in grasp, now allow the Lord to start the mending process. "Enter me, then; conceive a new, true life." Doesn't that sound great? A new, true life. A fresh start.

"Soak me in your laundry and I'll come out clean, scrub me and I'll have a snow-white life. Tune me in to foot-tapping songs, set these once-broken bones to dancing. Don't look too close for blemishes, give me a clean bill of health. God, make a fresh start in me, shape a Genesis week from the chaos of my life. Don't throw me out with the trash, or fail to breathe holiness in me. Bring me back from gray exile, put a fresh wind in my sails! Give me a job teaching rebels your ways so the lost can find their way home. Commute my death sentence, God, my salvation God, and I'll sing anthems to your life-giving ways. Unbutton my lips, dear God; I'll let loose with your praise."

Though we feel pain and suffering, and though we don't see ourselves worthy we need to cling to Psalm 51. It's in these moments when we feel our dirtiest that we need to cling to this word. In these moments of that sharp pain, when we want to listen to indie music and stare out our windows, we need to instead seek God. Rid me off these habits, these thoughts, this weakness, this vice, this stronghold. Break these chains. Lord, just breathe life.

It's easy to spot blemishes. Faults. Screw ups. Mistakes. Momentary lapses of good judgment. I'm broken, but the Lord can heal my brokenness. You may be broken, but he can heal your brokenness. You may be from a legacy of sin but in the blink of an eye, his love can turn it all around. He gives us a fresh start. A Genesis week is within grasp. A fresh start that will clear the fog of chaos and devastation is yours. Just take it. Just ask. Pray. Lord, create in me a fresh start.

CHAPTER SEVEN

All Me

I like rap music. That may have shocked you because I'm an ordained minister and ministers only listen to the contemporary Christian station on Pandora. Now, before you label me a heathen, I will neither confirm nor deny that I listen to Drake. Supposedly, he has a song called, "All Me." I wouldn't know, I just heard this information from an acquaintance. But rumor has it, this song is about worldly success and how he and his fellow rappers came to acquire it. It was all them. No help. All them.

This was my anthem when I was playing football. Whether it was true or not, I always believed nobody believed in me and that I had something to prove. I put this chip on my shoulder and made worldly success my goal. Anything less than that was failure. I wanted people to know who I was. My life was all about me. I was an average football player in high school, small but I had good hands and could catch the ball. After my senior season, a few small universities were willing to give me a chance to play at the next level. I eventually signed with a small Christian school in Eastern Kentucky. In my mind, my success was because of me—not my coaches, not my dad who spent hours every day playing catch with me, definitely not God. I did this on my own even though nobody thought I could. Drake was always playing in the background of my mind.

This poisonous mindset not only affected my football life, as I often fought with teammates, but it affected my relationships as well. Selfishness and arrogance would be two good words to sum it up, although I never would have admitted that at the time.

We see throughout the Bible that we as people, followers of Christ or not, are likened to sheep. And that struck me as odd. Psalm 23 starts off, "The Lord is my shepherd." (ESV). So if he is the shepherd, that obviously makes us sheep. Why sheep? Sheep really aren't that cool. Just pause and think, have you ever seen a sheep do anything cool? Have you ever seen sheep fight? They have no fangs or claws or anything. Have you ever heard of the Fighting Sheep? No, because sheep would be a terrible mascot. They just are not intimidating. I like tattoos and I do not know a single person with a tattoo of a sheep. Sheep don't lead revivals. In fact, sheep are very bad leaders. Why didn't he choose something cooler like a panther or say, "The Lord is my commander and I am his warrior?" That'd be a super dope psalm. But sheep are kind of stupid. They can't even bathe themselves. So why are we likened to sheep? Okay okay, yeah we aren't stupid all the time. And we can bathe ourselves, but I understand the point Jesus is trying to make. We need a shepherd.

But why? Most of us say, "I've got this covered God. I don't want to be a sheep. I want to be a lion. Lions do whatever they want, when they want to." Well that's the problem, we all want to do what we want, when we want. It's all about us. But more often than not, we find ourselves in a jam and it's usually our fault. Or maybe you haven't yet. You think you've got it all together and you're doing fine. So you're 100% in control of your emotions? Never in a bad mood? Never snap off on anyone? So you're on good terms with everyone? Every relationship you have ever had was great and even your ex's have nothing bad to say about you? You have no fears? No fear of failure? You don't need any forgiveness? You've never lied, cheated, done one thing wrong?

So if my calculations are correct, we cannot control our emotions all the time under all circumstances. Not every relationship we've ever had was perfect. We have fears, and sometimes we just come up short.

Well when I put it that way, sounds like we could all use a shepherd. So what exactly does that mean? What does it mean to have a shepherd? It means to have guidance and direction, protection, and at times discipline and correction. Yeah, you can tweet that if you want.

In the psalm, we read a metaphor where David writes about how God anoints his head with oil. As a kid, I pictured God pouring oil on some bald guy. Why the guy was bald, I do not know. But as I got older, I knew there had to be another meaning behind this. I read up on old customs and read that the sheep would often get cuts or injuries throughout the day while out in the fields, so if the shepherd was a good shepherd, he would get down to the dirty, smelly sheep's level and anointed the sheep with oil in order to protect the sheep's wounds from getting infected. I believe you and I walk through life and we get a lot of cuts and injuries. We may lose our jobs, we may lose our friends, and we may lose our money. Sometimes life is like Ronda Rousey and before you know it, you find yourself in an arm bar and the referee won't stop the fight even though you're tapping out. But if God is your shepherd, our God is so good, he's already anointed us. We don't have to tap out because we're already protected. We're protected from infection and sin that would try to come against us.

Another reason the shepherd anoints the sheep is, I heard a pastor say, flies would often go up inside of the sheep's brain and lay eggs and they would eventually hatch, causing the sheep constant torment and agony. The torment would fester and fester and the sheep would be found banging their heads on rocks in an attempt to alleviate the pain. Just think about that for a minute. Does that sound like you? Hopefully you don't literally have flies in your head, but do you ever allow negativity to fester in your head? Do you allow negative thoughts to dictate your actions? Do you allow the things people say about you to fester and eventually boil over? Do you put a chip on your own shoulder and feel like you have something to prove? Ultimately we're just going to keep banging our heads on rocks trying to alleviate the pain. Nothing in this world can alleviate the pain, and ultimately it'll just exacerbate the problem. I can assure you, banging its head on the rock did not help the sheep. Our pain is alleviated when we allow the shepherd to anoint us. And by that I mean when we allow the Lord into our life as not just our savior, or our supernatural Snuggie, but as our protector.

FINDING JESUS IN THE DISH ROOM

When I was pursuing my football dreams, I had isolated myself and wouldn't listen to anybody. During my high school career, I had several concussions, broken my collar bone twice, and had several other injuries. My mama was always praying and fasting for me and she told me that football wasn't my future and God had something even better planned for me. And I always felt convicted when I would go to church. Every time the pastor gave an altar call, my heart would start beating fast and my palms would get sweaty and my stomach would turn but I had too much pride to get out of my seat. It was this constant spiritual tug-of-war with Jesus. But in my mind, mama and God didn't know what they were talking about because football was my future. I wouldn't listen and eventually the time came for me to report to camp for summer practice and begin my college career, but it wasn't long before my world came crashing down. I suffered another concussion at practice and didn't know up from down, left from right, what my mama's name was, or what number came after five. I went to several neurologists and the consensus was that football was done for me or I'd be risking permanent brain damage. This was a devastating blow for me. Someone just hit this self-proclaimed Superman with a ton of kryptonite. Before I knew it, I was living back home, waking up every day feeling like a failure and trying to live with the symptoms that followed my concussion. Sitting on the toilet (I know this is like my third reference to sitting on the toilet, sorry, just keeping it real) without falling off was a challenge for me. I was devastated and depressed. And my mama never rubbed it in, but she knew she was right. I just wouldn't listen. To her or God. God had a plan for me and it wasn't football.

In the twenty-third psalm there is a phrase, "your rod and staff comfort me." This became real to me. I read that back in the day, if a sheep started to wander away from the other sheep, the shepherd would keep an eye on it and let it do its own thing for a while. Sounds like us sometimes, huh? We begin to wander a bit too far away. We know we shouldn't be out late on Saturday night because we have church in the morning, but we stay out anyway and we end up showing up late to the eleven o'clock service. Then we miss a Sunday. Then we miss a few Sundays. Next thing you know you aren't in church at all and you're living in the world and bam, you feel the rod and staff "comfort" you. Once the sheep got too far away, the shepherd would hit the sheep on the leg with his staff sometimes breaking the sheep's leg. Then he would just leave it laying there in pain and agony and say, "There, that'll teach you." No! He wouldn't leave it, he would pick it up and take care of its injuries and bring him back to the flock. He let the sheep wander but when it got too far, he did what was necessary. He corrected the sheep in order to protect it. Now, I'm not saying that Jesus wants to break your legs or hit you with a shepherd's rod (although it may feel that way sometimes). But he is so good and so merciful, and he loves you so much that he wants to save you from things you don't even know you need saving from. He may shut a door that you desperately wanted to walk through. He may not let you get into that relationship with that person you want to be with. He may let you wander and then get hit by a two-hundred-fifty-pound linebacker, but that doesn't mean he doesn't love you. He disciplines and corrects you because he loves you! So metaphorically speaking, you may have just gotten a nice good swat with his staff and your leg is hurting pretty bad or maybe it's just your ego but just know it was from a place of love and he isn't just going to leave you there, in whatever situation you find yourself in, to suffer. Like the shepherd with his sheep, the good shepherd is going to dust you off, pick you up, and bring you back to the flock. And next time you think about wandering off, hopefully you will, like the sheep, remember the correction and choose to stay close to the good shepherd and his love and mercy that never fail.

— CHAPTER EIGHT —

Girls Like Smoothies

One day a few years ago, my nephew Benjamin, who was six at the time, walked into my room and found me on the ground doing pushups. "Uncle Schuyler, what are you doing?"

"Well Ben, I'm doing pushups."

"Why?"

"Because they give you muscles. Girls like guys with muscles."

That must have sounded good to him because next thing I knew he was on the ground next to me struggling and straining to do a push up. After struggling for a few seconds, he stands up and asks, "Do girls like smoothies?"

Puzzled by this seemingly random question, I stopped and looked at him and he stared back very matter-of-fact. So I said, "Uh, yeah Ben, they do."

"Then I'll just make smoothies and girls will like me." Then he turned and walked out of the room and to this day has never done a push up. Mic drop.

Heck yeah, just make smoothies. It's much easier and girls will still like you. Win-win situation. Some people feel the need to obsess over their bodies, or diet extensively in order to feel attractive to the opposite sex but Ben has it figured out. You don't have to try so hard, it's easy to get women. Learn how to make smoothies. What is easier than that?

I think Ben, who at the age of six thought Jesus wore a dress, made a very profound theological statement. Girls like smoothies, but I think God does too. Some Christians and non-Christians for that matter, think that appeasing God is hard, or getting his attention is difficult so we overly strive for his attention and ultimately his approval or the non-believer thinks that it's such an impossible task that they just continue to live in sin and don't even try. Christians often try to be as attractive as possible and flex our spiritual muscles and we wake up at five every morning and read our Bibles for an hour, then we do a devotional, then pray for an hour, then we fast for a week, and yeah, all of that is fantastic but do you think that impresses God? Do you think God's up in Heaven like, "Hey Gabriel, get a load of this, he prayed for a whole hour today! Never seen that before." And do we think we need to impress him anyway to get his attention? Plus, all of that stuff is difficult to keep up every day. Give him a smoothie.

Serving God is easy. You shouldn't have to try and serve God. Being a Christian is not an act of striving or trying, it's just a way of life. We don't have to impress God. Like there's anything we could possibly do to impress him anyway. We don't have to try and make ourselves more attractive to him in order to get more love or blessings. He already loves you more than you can imagine and already has plans to bless you and prosper you.

On the opposite side of things, the non-believer sees the Christian life style as hard.

"Man, y'all gotta go to church every Sunday, and y'all can't drink, or smoke. Y'all can't have any fun. I just couldn't do all that. Living like that would be too hard."

Often, people have the mindset that it's too hard to be a Christian. It would be too difficult to live a lifestyle pleasing to God. As if God is up there and only loves people who don't drink or smoke and those alone are the requirements to get into Heaven. Like there are angels standing guard at the pearly gates with a breathalyzer and a pee cup and you have to pass both before he'll let you inside. I am in no way condoning the consumption of alcohol or the use of tobacco or marijuana. All I am saying is Christianity is not just about not doing those things, or making yourself more attractive or more lovable to God. He already loves you and there is nothing we could do in the first place to earn his love. He gives it freely because we are his children.

God has called us to be leaders by his standards, not by our standards. I know a lot of us see the pastor with the big stage, the microphone, and a crowd of twenty thousand people as a leader and we think that's how you know you've arrived. But we don't see the behind the scenes that got them there. A lot of us want the spotlight and assume that's the only way God can use you. Or that's the only way to impress God. Yeah reaching thousands of people is great but what about reaching one? We think it takes a revival to impress God? Well it says in Luke that the angels rejoice when just one lost soul accepts Jesus. I don't think it's possible to impress him but I know it's possible to move him. And that's by following him. By being a servant leader and washing feet, so to speak. I hate feet so I probably won't literally do that but when Jesus washed his disciple's feet, it wasn't leadership by this world's standards. He was showing us something deeper than that.

"Jesus knew that the Father had put him in complete charge of everything, that he came from God and was on his way back to God. So he got up from the supper table, set aside his robe, and put on an apron. Then he poured water into a basin and began to wash the feet of the disciples, drying them with his apron. When he got to Simon Peter, Peter said, 'Master, *you* wash *my* feet?'

Jesus answered, 'You don't understand now what I'm doing, but it will be clear enough to you later.'

Peter persisted, 'You're not going to wash my feet—ever!'

Jesus said, 'If I don't wash you, you can't be part of what I'm doing.'

'Master!' said Peter. 'Not only my feet, then. Wash my hands! Wash my head!'

Jesus said, 'If you've had a bath in the morning, you only need your feet washed now and you're clean from head to toe. My concern, you understand, is holiness, not hygiene. So now you're clean. But not every one of you.' (He knew who was betraying him. That's why he said, 'Not every one of you.') After he had finished washing their feet, he took his robe, put it back on, and went back to his place at the table.

Then he said, 'Do you understand what I have done to you? You address me as 'Teacher' and 'Master,' and rightly so. That is what I am. So if I, the Master and Teacher, washed your feet, you must now wash each other's feet. I've laid down a pattern for you. What I've done, you do. I'm only pointing out the obvious. A servant is not ranked above his master; an employee doesn't give orders to the employer. If you understand what I'm telling you, act like it—and live a blessed life.'" John 13:3-17, (MSG).

This was obviously unexpected. I mean, come on, this was Jesus, the greatest leader in human history. This guy preaches to thousands of people on mountains (Matthew 5-7), heals blind eyes (Mark 8:22-25, John 9), raises dead people from the grave (it's not as creepy as it sounds I promise, check out Luke 17:11-25, Luke 8:41, 42, 49-55, John 11:1-44), turns water into wine (Jesus liked to party, John 2:1-11), and here he was washing his disciples feet. This was crazy. But what he was showing us was that leadership is serving others. You want to move God, wash someone's feet. Not literally, please. But be compassionate, serve others above yourself, love each other, pray for the sick. And then don't tweet about it or post it on your Facebook. If you're seeking to impress this world, you're not seeking God. God wants us to seek him humbly; even the Son of Man came, not to be served, but to serve. It's that easy. Heck, it's easier than making a smoothie. Our culture has become so jaded that if you smile at someone, you get a weird look back, and if we see someone we know, instead of saying "Hi," we look down or pull out our phones. If you want to move God, be loving and kind in this world that thinks smiling and saying "Hi" is weird. Offer to pray for someone hurting today. Give a word of encouragement and lift someone up. Washing feet and making smoothies is how you move God.

God likes smoothies. Show love to your neighbor, forgive somebody even though they didn't apologize, show compassion to that homeless guy you just passed by. Show mercy and be gracious. Love, forgiveness, compassion, mercy, and grace. Throw all that in the blender together and God will be pleased.

── CHAPTER NINE ──

Scandalous Grace

When I was in high school, I was on the school news team. We would often make short little skits and funny videos to fill in the space between boring school announcements. One in particular stands out to me. A couple of my friends and I decided to run up and hug random people we saw walking down the halls while we filmed with a hidden camera. The reactions were as you could imagine: quite hilarious. Everybody flinched or got really awkward. I actually had a janitor stop me because she thought I was assaulting someone. Nobody knows what to do with a hug. Especially one they did nothing to deserve. Here's where I'm going with this: Jesus wants to walk up and give us a nice, random hug and we flinch and pull away because we feel we did nothing to deserve it. The fact of the matter is we often feel like he should slap us across the face or point and laugh, but he definitely should not hug us.

We're all human. We're all bound at some point to mess up. Some more than others. Some are lost in their sin. Broken. But as I read the Bible, I see that God has a tendency to use broken vessels. Rarely is the hero of a Bible story the guy who has it all together. The person God uses is the underdog, the fisherman, the unqualified, the thug, the prostitute, the alcoholic, the murdering adulterer. Now you probably don't feel too bad about yourself, huh? Keep in mind, they were repentant and forgiven, but when they first encountered Jesus and his infinite goodness and grace, they had issues, they were broken. Sinners. Human.

"It wasn't so long ago that you were mired in that old stagnant life of sin. You let the world, which doesn't know the first thing about living, tell you how to live. You filled your lungs with polluted unbelief, and then exhaled disobedience. We all did it, all of us doing what we felt like doing when we felt like doing it, all of us in the same boat. It's a wonder god didn't lose his temper and do away with the whole lot of us. Instead, immense in mercy and with an incredible love, he embraced us. He took our sin-dead lives and made us alive in Christ. He did all this on his own, with no help from us! Then he picked us up and set us down in the highest heaven in company with Jesus our Messiah." Ephesians 2:1-6, (MSG).

When I was washing dishes, I worked with a girl who didn't exactly believe what I did. She was "searching" for something and hadn't quite found what she was looking for. As sad as it is, her situation isn't uncommon. In fact, it's far too common. She loved people and had a good heart but there was something missing. Our paths really crossed when one day she came into the dish room and mockingly asked, "Hey dish boy, are you going to help me find Jesus?" (Hence the title of the book). This sarcastic question thrilled me. I took this jab as an opportunity to evangelize. Upon weeks of conversations, finally she said to me, "I've done too much for Jesus to love me." This was it. This was the wall that needed to be broken down.

I feel like her story is the same as a lot of people's. "I've done too much." "I've done too much bad." "I don't deserve his grace." She had never heard about the real grace of God. The infinite goodness that he wants to pour out into her life. She didn't believe it. This grace in Ephesians 2 is "too good to be true." It's scandalous. It doesn't make sense. Exactly. That's our God. He is scandalous. His love and grace is ridiculous. She was right, she didn't deserve it. I don't deserve it. You don't deserve it. But his grace is not a parole deal, Jesus is not our parole officer. His grace is not dependent on us being good people. News flash, we aren't. We are sinful. We couldn't earn this even if we tried. So it's even more ridiculous for us as the body of Christ to put ourselves on a pedestal so much so that people look down on themselves because we try to put ourselves so high up.

The Bible says it best, "You let the world, which doesn't know the first thing about living, tell you how to live. You filled your lungs with polluted unbelief, and then exhaled disobedience." My friend wasn't unique in this regard. She let her circumstances, her pain, the world dictate how she would live her life. The world is polluted. The culture is broken. So that was the air she was breathing in. Maybe this is the air you are breathing into your lungs. Maybe you too are letting this broken world call the shots and determine how you live your life. In listening to the world, you are in direct opposition of God. Therefore, when you breathe in this world, when you take in what it has to offer, you breathe out disobedience. When you take part in the desires of your flesh, you are disobeying God and therefore missing out on his perfect will for your life. Good thing I'm not God because if you turned your back on me and all I was trying to do was help you, I'd say, "Forget you. Just wait, you'll regret turning your back on me." And then I'd be taking selfies in Heaven on the day of judgement for everyone to see on my Instagram. I'd be tweeting at my haters. But thank God that is not the God we serve. This concept of trying to earn God's grace or thinking it's something we can deserve is totally in opposition with the Gospel. This concept implies we have to "do," but our faith says "done." As in, it is done for us. The work is done for us. The sacrifice has been made so now we get this free gift of salvation and love and a scandalous kind of grace. It was nothing we earned in the first place. It was not given to us because we deserved it or because we were good. It was given to us because we are bad but he is good.

If you aren't familiar with the Bible, Jesus often taught moral lessons through stories, or parables as they're called. One of my favorites is the parable of the prodigal son. I'm sure you're familiar with it.

"Then he said, 'There was once a man who had two sons. The younger said to his father, 'Father, I want right now what's coming to me.'

So the father divided the property between them. It wasn't long before the younger son packed his bags and left for a distant country. There, undisciplined and dissipated, he wasted everything he had. After he had gone through all his money, there was a bad famine all through that country and he began to hurt. He signed on with a citizen there who assigned him to his fields to slop the pigs. He was so hungry he would have eaten the corncobs in the pig slop, but no one would give him any.

That brought him to his senses. He said, 'All those farmhands working for my father sit down to three meals a day, and here I am starving to death. I'm going back to my father. I'll say to him, Father, I've sinned against God, I've sinned before you; I don't deserve to be called your son. Take me on as a hired hand.' He got right up and went home to his father.

When he was still a long way off, his father saw him. His heart pounding, he ran out, embraced him, and kissed him. The son started his speech: 'Father, I've sinned against God, I've sinned before you; I don't deserve to be called your son ever again.'

But the father wasn't listening. He was calling to the servants, 'Quick. Bring a clean set of clothes and dress him. Put the family ring on his finger and sandals on his feet. Then get a grain-fed heifer and roast it. We're going to feast! We're going to have a wonderful time! My son is here—given up for dead and now alive! Given up for lost and now found!' And they began to have a wonderful time." Luke 15:11-32, (MSG).

What gets me every time is the father's reaction. We have this arrogant kid who wants his inheritance early so he can go waste it on booze and women and once it's all gone he decides he wants to come back home. We read that the father spotted him from a long way off. So evidently, the father had been looking and waiting for his son to return. I feel like this paints a good picture of our Heavenly Father. We took our inheritance and squandered it. And in our shame and guilt, we began our search for something more. And he saw us wandering around a long way off because he was looking for us and waiting.

But back to the story, the father, seeing his son, hops off his porch and literally runs to embrace him. It's a wonder he didn't trip running in his robe and sandals. The cool thing about that is that men back in that time period and culture did not run. It was undignified for him to run, but he didn't care. Dignified or not, he runs to his son, overlooks his failures and shortcomings, and embraces him. Much like our Heavenly Father does with us. Jesus celebrates when we come home and embrace him.

I can see the angels asking Jesus, "What's the big deal about this one? Schuyler's arrogant and foolish." And Jesus says very compassionately, "He'll grow out of it. He's my son and I love him and he's come home."

So even when we've thrown away our inheritance and indulged in sin, God runs to us and embraces us and clothes us in the finest robes and shows us scandalous grace.

For some reason, a lot of us have this default view of God as this angry old man, hollering at us to get off his lawn. We have this image of this angry deity when in fact it's quite the opposite and he isn't intimidated by your sin the way we seem to be. The reason people feel like they've done too much bad is when we find out about their bad, our response is usually, "Whoa, you did what?" And then we proceed to pat ourselves on the back because at least we're not doing that. The story that sticks out to me is found in John chapter 8. This story starts with a group of godly, God-fearing, religious vigilantes dragging a woman before Jesus who they caught in the act of sexual sin. According to the law of that day, she should have been condemned and stoned to death for her sin. So they ask Jesus what they should do with her, expecting him to uphold this law and be the first to pick up and throw a stone. Oftentimes, that's how we picture Jesus handling our own sin. We think he's just waiting to stone us for our sin, but his response is the epitome of grace and mercy. Jesus doesn't pick up any stones but instead, he challenges the accusers with a simple yet profound statement. "Let the one of you who hasn't ever sinned throw the first stone."

I'm sure it got really awkward at that point as they all stood there speechless and all you could hear was the sound of stones hitting the dirt as the men dropped their stones and one by one left the woman there with Jesus. Jesus then asks her, "Where are your accusers? Not even one of them condemns you, huh?"

"No, Lord."

"I don't either. Go and sin no more."

I've noticed we are often harsher in our judgement and quicker to do so than God is. We hold back grace and we forget how freely it was given to us. We catch someone in sin and immediately we want to grab our pitchforks and torches and chase them out of town "in the name of Jesus." The fact of the matter is, we have all, in one way or another, sinned against God. So who are we to cast the first stone? The only person who has any right to do so refused.

― CHAPTER TEN ―

The Gospel Pep Talk

Psalm 23. Everyone knows this passage. Maybe not the whole thing but they know the gist. Maybe because of the Coolio song. No? Yeah, me either, I'm a man of God; I don't listen to rap music. But regardless, it is, in my opinion, one of the most powerful passages in all of scripture. And the most beautiful thing about it is the author's journey, mistakes, and conquests that were behind the writing of the psalm. This was written by a man who had been through a lot. This was not written by a man who had it all together. This psalm is a great picture of emotion. David was full of faults, he gave into temptation, yet God was still able to use him to write possibly the most influential, beautiful articulation of the Gospel. So do not think for a second that God cannot use you. Do not think you've done too much bad for God to use you for something good. Don't think he cannot turn your brokenness around and give you life to glorify him.

"God, my shepherd! I don't need a thing. You have bedded me down in lush meadows, you find me quiet pools to drink from. True to your word, you let me catch my breath and send me in the right direction. Even when the way goes through Death Valley, I'm not afraid when you walk at my side Your trusty shepherd's crook makes me feel secure. You serve me a six-course dinner right in front of my enemies. You revive my drooping head; my cup brims with blessing. Your beauty and love chase after me every day of my life. I'm back home in the house of God for the rest of my life." (MSG).

Verse one says, "The lord is my shepherd. I lack nothing." You may feel like you have absolutely nothing or you may look at your life and see it headed down a dead end, but if you have Jesus you have all that you could ever need.

In verse four, it says, "Even when the way goes through Death Valley, I'm not afraid when you walk at my side." The English Standard Version says, "Even though I walk through the valley of the shadow of death, I will fear no evil for you are with me." When I read this psalm and this verse in particular, I can see David staring at his reflection in his mirror, pep talking himself. We have all been there. You didn't get a good night's sleep, up tossing and turning all night, you feel like hell. A sleepless night of thoughts driving you crazy, replaying memories and remembering your shortcomings. Staring at his reflection trying to pep himself up, he declares, "Whether you like it or not David, God is your shepherd. I will walk on through the valley. I will not pitch my tent and set up camp in the valley. I will not make s'mores in the valley. I will not make myself comfortable in the valley. I will not wallow in my self-pity. I will walk on through. There are better days ahead of me despite what my situation and circumstance may be telling me." See, David understood something a lot of us as Christians have a hard time grasping. Even though you may not want to hear it, the truth is still the truth, whether you like it or not. God is for you, not against you. This kind of validates that Christian cliché person. "I heard about your financial situation and I wanted to tell you that God put all the stars in the universe so he can take care of you." Thanks. Very helpful. I don't want a star, I'd like a couple bucks; I want a McDouble, and my rent's due. The fact of the matter is, that person is right. The God of the universe put the stars in the sky, designed the entire world, designed you, and wants what is best for you. You, this tiny little speck in this enormous universe. If he can build and construct galaxies with no effort, how easy would it be for him to provide for you? He has plans for you, according to Jeremiah 29; he has plans to prosper you and give you a future and a hope. Things may look bleak now, you may be in a valley, but remember what his word says. Remember the truth in the words. Take hold of them and speak them over your life. The Lord is your shepherd and you lack nothing.

I had a friend I met while living in Louisville. The guy was a walking Bible. I've never met a man who could recite scripture like he could. In class, he would sit there and fidget uncomfortably, smoking his e-cig, dying for the teacher to stop talking so he could begin to argue. And he rarely lost. You couldn't tell him anything because he already knew it. He had all the head knowledge. He also had an addiction to heroin, meth, and cocaine. Because of this, he had lost everything: his family, friends, and his job. He was depressed and suicidal. He had all the head knowledge, but couldn't apply it in his own life. He knew Jeremiah 29:11 in his head but it wasn't in his heart. He knew Psalm 23 but he didn't know the shepherd. You may not be a drug addict. You may have a seemingly simpler problem but with the same crippling effects. You may have a problem dealing with fear or anxiety. Pep talk yourself with 2 Timothy 1:7 and remind yourself that that spirit of fear is not from God, but instead he gave you power to overcome, love, and a sound mind. You may struggle seeing your worth. Remind yourself that you are fearfully and wonderfully made. Pep talk yourself with 2 Corinthians 5:17 and know that it doesn't matter what you did in the past, it cannot affect your future with Christ because you are a new creation. But it isn't enough to know the words, they need to be permanently tattooed on your heart. When life becomes overwhelming or when that voice in your head tells you you'll always be an addict, or reminds you about all your unpaid bills, or starts to remind you of your past failures, counter it with the word of God. Whether you like it or not, his word remains true, and you are more than a conqueror through him.

CHAPTER ELEVEN

God, Can You Hear Me?

I was in a chapter of my life, or "a season" as your pastor calls it, that wasn't making a lot of sense. I felt led by God to pack up and leave my comfortable life, my family, my friends, all two of them, and move from rural west Kentucky to Louisville, Kentucky. I imagined all the great things God was going to use me to do. I was going to conquer the world, starting with Louisville, all for God's glory of course. Also, my girlfriend at the time was living in Louisville (which in hindsight might have had a lot to do with feeling "called" to this particular city). But it wasn't long before reality set in. My bills are due and the money's not coming in. I'm going days without eating. There's no heat in my apartment. I'm not making an impact here. I feel stagnant. I miss my family. I miss my comfortable life, I miss my $8 an hour job washing dishes. Woe is me. Then my girl dumps me within the first two months of my moving there. The point is, I'm not seeing God move in my life. Where's Jesus at? I'm down on my knees praying and finally I ask him, "Jesus, can you hear me? I'm here because of you and so far this is a disaster. You're not answering me." His answer to me changed everything. "Schuyler, can *you* hear *me*?" I felt so humbled and slightly embarrassed. I had made my calling all about me, rather than him. I felt God calling me to the ministry and then I said, "I'll take it from here." Instead, I should've said "Okay Jesus, what's next?" I know from experience, we as Christians, or as non-Christians for that matter, question if God hears us. The answer is yes, he does. He hears you just fine. But just because he hears us, doesn't mean he's obligated to answer every prayer request we have, and thank God for that. I can't tell you how many times Jesus saved me from my own prayer requests. But the question isn't about his ability to hear us, but our ability to hear him.

    John 10 says, "The shepherd walks right up to the gate. The gatekeeper opens the gate to him and the sheep recognize his voice. He calls his own sheep by name and leads them out. When he gets them all out, he leads them and they follow because they are familiar with his voice… I am the Good Shepherd." (MSG). To really understand this, I had to understand the context of it. Back in the day, say there were ten shepherds with one hundred sheep each, making a total of one thousand. At the end of the day, all ten shepherds would bring their one hundred sheep to one location and put them in one fenced in area and nine shepherds would go back to town and one would stay and watch over the sheep for the night. The next day, they would return and one by one they would enter the gate and see one thousand sheep. The shepherd would then call *his* sheep. At that moment, it didn't matter if the sheep was black, white, grazing with the cool sheep, or grazing alone; the sheep would hear their shepherd and follow him. What God is saying here is, "I am the Good Shepherd so get to know my voice." The sheep weren't concerned with what they were doing or making their name known. The sheep heard their shepherd's voice and listened.

Too many of us hear his voice and are too busy doing our own thing to listen. We've got this life thing figured out. The sheep didn't say, "Hold on shepherd, I'm too busy grazing. As a matter of fact, I'll hang back here today. And Jim was telling me his shepherd takes them down to the good valley and the grass is a lot greener there so tomorrow I'll probably roll with them. Later, bro." Now I know sheep can't talk, but you get the idea. Sometimes we think our ideas are better than God's ideas. God's calling but we aren't hearing it. The grass over there is too appealing. We claim God isn't listening but he is. We aren't. We tell God to use us and send us anywhere but then give him conditions.

Us: "God use me! Send me! I want to pastor a church."
God: "Go to Africa and dig a well."
Us: "God I don't think you heard me right."
God: "Go to Africa and dig a well.
Us: "I want to be a Pastor. Why aren't things working out?"
God: "Because I called you to be a missionary."
Us: "God, why aren't you helping me?!"
God: sigh *face palm*

So the problem isn't that he isn't answering, sometimes it's just the answer we don't want to hear and we aren't listening. I've found that when God is "silent" in my life, it has nothing to do with his flaws but rather, flaws in myself. Often times, we take the calling God gave us and we say, "thanks" and we take off. We think we have it all figured out but it's a harsh wakeup call when we realize that we need God through all the steps. Yes, Jesus has a plan for your life, and yes, you may already have an idea of what that is, but that doesn't mean he needs to take a back seat and just go along for the ride. He needs to continuously be in the driver's seat and that means listening to his voice and allowing him to guide you.

CHAPTER TWELVE

The Carpenter and the Crook

As a Christian, you should be surrounded by brokenness. Confused? That's the problem. Let me explain. Nowadays, we in our Christian culture have made Christianity about good deeds and being better than everyone else, hanging out with other Christians and being comfortable in our bubble. We've made Christianity into an obligation to feed the hungry once a month and halfheartedly read our Bibles at night, and to go to church more to socialize than to hear the word of God. But the thing is, we feel like this is enough to put ourselves on a pedestal, in a position to look down on everyone else. We aren't changing the world; we are staying away from it. This isn't the example Jesus left us with. Who did Jesus hang out with? Who did Jesus associate with? Who did he spend his time with? The answer is drunks, prostitutes, and tax collectors, most notably Zacchaeus.

As the story goes, Jesus entered Jericho and was making his way through the town. And this little man named Zacchaeus heard that Jesus was coming through and he as a Jew would have been familiar with the prophecies and knew the Messiah would one day come. So he decided to check this out. He was like I mentioned before, smaller in stature and couldn't see over the crowd so he decided to climb up in a tree to see what all the fuss was about.

As Jesus passes by the tree, he stops and calls him by name, "Zacchaeus! Come on down. I'm coming over to your place."

Zacchaeus in his excitement, jumped out of the tree and took him to his house. But much like today, all the righteous people began to grumble. "Who does Jesus think he is? Associating with that notorious sinner?!"

But as they were judging and talking under their breath, Zacchaeus was with Jesus and said, "I'll give away half of my wealth in order to help the poor and if I've cheated anyone I will give them back four times as much."

Jesus said, "Today salvation has come to your home. The Son of Man came to seek and save the lost."

All of this can be found in Luke 19:1-10.

So who is this guy exactly? Zacchaeus was a pimp. He was "quite rich," the Bible says in one translation. Zacchaeus was ballin'. Zacchaeus was also a cheat, and a tax collector for the Roman government who ruled Israel at the time, so he was also hated by his fellow Jews. His job was to collect the taxes from his people and turn it over to the Roman government. His income was whatever he could embezzle and cheat out of the people after he paid what was owed to the government. This was the guy stealing candy from babies. So we have a corrupt tax collector cheating his own people, God's chosen people, so by all accounts Jesus should have stayed clear of this crook.

We in our religion today would have looked down on this guy and steered away from coming into contact with this no good thief. So Jesus, being perfect, should've definitely overlooked this guy and sat down and talked with the priests about how sinful our world was and got a prayer group together and huddled up and prayed for revival in this wicked world. Nope. Jesus not only talked with this guy, he called him by name and fellowshipped with this guy and ate with him at his home. Jesus just showed up and showed love with no condemnation. His nose wasn't in the air as he ignored this lowly sinner while he walked on his way to do important God things. Jesus embraced this man and talked to him like a friend. He spoke from a place of love. He knew what Zacchaeus did for a living. He knows all about this guy and how he makes his money. But he didn't judge him. He didn't reject him. He loved him. And in doing something as simple and easy as hanging out with him, Jesus changed his heart. After a meal with Jesus, we see this greedy, embezzling tax collector decide to give away his fortune to the poor and all those he has cheated. He's about to be broke and it doesn't matter because he now knows the Messiah. Zacchaeus repented and salvation came to him and his home. There was no worship team, there was no prayer group, and there was no preacher with a long message on repentance and salvation. There was a carpenter from a nobody town, shining the light of the Gospel, and that alone caused Zacchaeus to ask forgiveness of his sins and become a follower of Jesus. So my point to all this is: we all know a Zacchaeus. And my question to you is, are you reaching him? Are you making an effort to get to know him? Or do you pull out your cell phone and pretend to text someone as they pass you in the hall? Do you leave when he shows up to the same place you are? Ask yourself, is your life a shining light for the Gospel? Is there one more soul going to Heaven when eternity comes because you made the effort to reach the lost? Where there was brokenness, were you there? Where there was darkness, did you bring the light? Where there was death, did you bring life? Do you know any pimps, or any drug dealers? Alcoholics? No? That's a problem. There should be no alleyway, corner, liquor store, club, bar, college campus, office, work space, that isn't being impacted by the Gospel. Once we have the revelation that we are all disciples and our job as Christian is to spread the Gospel, it changes everything. Lives are changed, things won't ever be the same. Jesus was just a carpenter from a small town according to this world.

You don't have to be ordained, you don't have to be a pastor, and you don't have to have any certain title to be a walking revival. You just need to realize that you are called by the God of the universe to impact every person you come across. You may just be a student or just a stay at home mom, or just a dishwasher. Your worldly title may not say much, but your title doesn't define you. God defines you. This world's label does not give you identity, God does. And he has called you to be a disciple and to be a witness for our risen savior. Our jobs as students, stay-at-home moms, and dishwashers are not just to do our jobs but to do our jobs in a way that glorifies God. Every move we make and every step we take should point to Jesus.

In John 4, we find Jesus again causing headlines and controversy when he sat with the women at the well. You see, she was a Samaritan. Back in those days, Jews would not be seen talking to Samaritans. So that in itself was enough to cause double takes. But this woman in particular is, well, to put it nicely, quite promiscuous. So the fact that Jesus was sitting with her having a conversation was straight up ripe for juicy gossip. The tabloids would have had a field day. But Jesus didn't care. He knew he was doing God's work and he knew the sick were the ones that needed a doctor. And not just the literal sick, but those sick in their sin.

So Jesus uncovered her sin: she had had five previous husbands and the man she currently lived with was not her husband. He then proceeded to point his finger in her face, wagged it, saying, "thou shalt not," made her feel bad, made her fall on her face, repent, and beg for forgiveness and then, and only then, could she look upon him and his glory. No, quite the opposite actually. He proceeded to tell her that he is living water and that those who drink from him will not thirst but will live forever. He answered all her problems with that statement. He answered all your problems as well. You see, we are the women at the well. Living in our sinful life, looking for love, Jesus tells us to look to him for he is true life. He didn't point out her sin from a place of condemnation but rather from a place of love. He made her aware of it, and told her about true life. A lot of times, we want to point out other people's sin and condemn them when in fact we should remind them that Jesus loves them so much, even in their sin, that he doesn't want them to stay that way. And before we point and wag our disapproving finger in the face of sinners, we need to remember that we are all sinners saved only by grace. Yet even though we are sinners, we are redeemed and set free and that comes with a responsibility. A responsibility to not keep this to ourselves. This salvation comes with a responsibility to reach the lost, to turn over every rock, run down every street, tell every neighbor about the goodness of God, about his love and mercy, about his grace and salvation. Our job is to find the broken and point them to Jesus Christ. Our job is not to pick and choose who hears the good news. Our job isn't to hide in the comfort of our church sanctuaries. Our job is to change the world by living in it and not just living, but living for Christ. Our job is to exemplify what it means to be a Christian, which is ultimately following Jesus. Our job is to boldly proclaim our testimonies. Our job is to be shining lights for the Gospel wherever we go. So ultimately people, should be tweeting about you, and gossiping, and talking under their breath because of the things you are doing. It will make no sense why you are sitting with that women at the well. You'll probably get a few weird looks. But rest easy knowing you are doing God's work.

CHAPTER THIRTEEN

Even When You're Laying on Your Couch Alone, and Broke in the West End on Thanksgiving, God is Still Good

Happiness. We all want to be happy and live happy lives and, for the most part, we believe happiness comes from good circumstances. We're happy when things go right. And why wouldn't we be? Things going right is awesome. But what about when things don't go right? Or when they go terribly wrong? We often seek to change our circumstances thinking that'll fix the problem. We begin to believe that changing our current situation will be the remedy for our unhappiness. If you're single, you seek a spouse. When that doesn't do it for you, you get a divorce and try to find someone else. You think kids will help, but kids are loud and puke on you, so that's not the key to happiness either. You think getting rich will do it, but you get rich (I do not know from experience, just what I've heard), and evidently even money doesn't ensure you happiness.

The Christian life proposes a sort of remedy for this constant struggle to find happiness. Jesus says in Mark, "If anyone would come after me, let him deny himself and take up his cross and follow me. For whoever would save his life will lose it, but whoever loses his life for my sake and the gospel's will save it." (ESV). Jesus made a similar statement in the book of Matthew in the Sermon on the Mount, where he contrasted the pagans, who sought after the material comforts of life, with believers, who Jesus advises to "seek first his kingdom and righteousness; and all these things shall be added unto you" found in Matthew 6:33 (ESV). So what Jesus is advising us to do is live a life free of self, to not live for our own personal fulfillment, and he will take care of us. The life of a Christian is a daily submission to the will of God. To say, "no" to selfish desires and ask instead that God's will be done. In denying ourselves, we bring to God every feeling, thought, action, desire, and relationship and ask the question, "Is this pleasing to you?" Because at the end of the day, our happiness boils down to selfishness. "I want this. I want that. I'll be happy when I get the promotion and I'm making more money." Most of our futile attempts at happiness are fueled by selfishness and our need for more. Jesus is saying, "Do not worry about all that, do not worrying about striving to make a name for yourself, or make more money, seek Me first and foremost and I'll help a brotha out." We may not get the promotion we want, but I personally, would rather make $7.25 an hour and it be blessed by God then make $100 an hour and be out of his will.

At the end of Paul's life, his circumstances were enough to break anyone's spirit. The Apostle Paul was at the point in his life where he should have been retired, coasting through the rest of his life off book sales, and relaxing by the pool. Instead of comfort and wealth, he was in a jail cell facing execution. Given the circumstances he found himself in, he would have had every right to be unhappy, but he never once complained. We don't find him questioning God, "Why me?! I've served you so faithfully and *this* is the situation I'm in?" We find him rejoicing in Philippians 1:18. Paul was able to have this mindset not because he had mastered Jedi mind tricks or took up meditation or yoga; it was because he was able to put into practice the words of Jesus Christ and denied himself for the sake of the Gospel. The circumstances surrounding his arrest would have been enough to make anybody mad, but not Paul. He was able to turn his prison into a mission field and had the revelation that happiness comes through proclaiming the Gospel in all situations. Even when we don't understand what's going on and even when he takes us out of our comfort zone, we have to trust God in all things and remain steadfast in our pursuit of expanding the good news that Jesus came and died for each and every one of us. Even you.

── CHAPTER FOURTEEN ──

Is Jesus in Your Boat?

Boat and anchor tattoos are a must in the hipster Christian starter pack, along with tight pants, a beard, and a goofy hairstyle (I happen to sport all the above save for the boat tattoo). But let's focus on the boat and anchor here for a chapter. Two of my favorite passages in the Bible include stormy oceans and the anchor holding everything in place despite the crashing waves. Turn with me in your bibles to Matthew chapter 14 and we'll begin reading at verse 22 and end on verse 32. When you're there say, "I'm there."

Verse 22 starts, "Immediately he made the disciples get into the boat and go before him to the other side, while he dismissed the crowds. And after he had dismissed the crowds, he went up on the mountain by himself to pray. When evening came, he was there alone, but the boat by this time was a long way from the land, beaten by the waves, for the wind was against them. And in the fourth watch of the night he came to them, walking on the sea. But when the disciples saw him walking on the sea, they were terrified, and said, 'It is a ghost!' and they cried out in fear. But immediately Jesus spoke to them, saying, 'Take heart; it is I. Do not be afraid.'

And Peter answered him, 'Lord, if it is you, command me to come to you on the water.' He said, 'Come.' So Peter got out of the boat and walked on the water and came to Jesus. But when he saw the wind, he was afraid, and beginning to sink he cried out, 'Lord, save me.' Jesus immediately reached out his hand and took hold of him, saying to him, 'O you of little faith, why did you doubt?' And when they got into the boat, the wind ceased. And those in the boat worshiped him, saying, 'Truly you are the Son of God.'" Matthew 14:22-32 (ESV).

My coworker was quiet. In a kitchen full of curse words and 90's rap music, it was already hard to get a word in, but my friend didn't even try. Of all the guys in the kitchen, he was the quietest. With headphones in, listening to sports radio, he would cook steaks like a master craftsman. At first, we didn't talk much; the big skull on his arm worked as a sort of repellant for small talk. The longer we worked together, a sort of friendship began to take shape. Although we talked more, I still knew very little about him. He would often mock my faith and would always try to change the subject if it was brought up. But one night, that changed. I had finished washing the last of the dishes for the night and instead of leaving, the two of us decided to hang out in the parking lot for a few minutes while he drank a beer. What began as small talk turned into a lot more. I soon learned the reason for his quiet demeanor and hostility toward my faith was years of heartache and anger. He had the "what kind of god" mentality as in, "What kind of god would allow the sweetest Christian women I know to suffer with cancer?" "What kind of god would allow a small boy to watch his two best friends die?" My friend was angry—angry at God, angry at life. And God was to blame for his past tragedies and present circumstances. "If God is so good, tell me why my life is so hard?"

I was scared. I didn't have the answers. I didn't know what to say that would make this all better. There is nothing I could say to make any difference in his life. But there is plenty that Jesus has said. Including Matthew chapter 14:22-32. You see, in the beginning, Jesus sent the disciples out ahead of him. Meaning he was not right there with them at the exact moment of the storm. He was God so he knew fully that he was sending them out into a storm. He was knowingly sending his friends, men he loved, into a dangerous situation. Let's look at this literally and metaphorically. Sometimes we face storms in life, and Jesus is fully aware of the situation we now face well ahead of time and still he allows us to go through it. But he didn't just leave the disciples to figure it out for themselves and struggle alone. He was passing by when he heard them cry out to him. He was going to just pass on by but he stopped. Maybe you're in a storm and God is passing by and he is just waiting for you to cry out to him. He wants to calm your storm, but you first have to reach out to him. First, we have to surrender, realize we are often powerless to change things and that we need a savior. Sometimes it seems like we're drowning but thank God Jesus walks on water. Peter's response to this situation is awesome. He asks Jesus to prove himself. "If it's you, let me walk out on the water." And guess what. He does. His trust in the Lord is now allowing him to do the impossible. When the story began, he was getting thrown around the boat in the midst of a storm, scared, tired, possibly questioning his faith, but when we finish the story, we see him walking on water holding onto Jesus. Yeah, he got scared, and began to sink, but guess who was right there to grab him. Jesus was there. And they got back into the boat and Jesus calmed the seas. So yeah, sometimes you'll experience pain and things you do not understand and yes, sometimes Jesus is allowing it to happen. But Jesus wants to calm your seas. He wants to calm the wind. But first, you have to invite him into your boat. For Peter, what started as one instance of fear and doubt, Jesus soon turned it into his defining moment. My friend invited Jesus into his boat that night and gave his life to the Lord in the parking lot of a bar with a Bud Light in his hand. God is good.

In Luke Chapter 8, we have another instance of Jesus telling the wind to shut up and the waves to chill, bro. Verses 22-25 say, "One day he got into a boat with his disciples, and he said to them, 'Let us go across to the other side of the lake.' So they set out, and as they sailed he fell asleep. And a windstorm came down on the lake, and they were filling with water and were in danger. And they went and woke him, saying, 'Master, Master, we are perishing!' And he awoke and rebuked the wind and the raging waves, and they ceased, and there was a calm. He said to them, 'Where is your faith?' And they were afraid, and they marveled, saying to one another, 'Who then is this, that he commands even winds and water, and they obey him?'" Luke 8:22-25 (ESV).

Now, I do not have a cool salvation story to go along with this one, but stay with me here. There is a terrible storm going on and the disciples are scared. Keep in mind his disciples were experienced fisherman so if they were scared, they had plenty of reason. Maybe you're experiencing a storm that is scary and you have every right to worry, panic even. But in this story Jesus was in the boat. So wait a minute. Jesus is in the boat and they're still hitting a storm? Yes. Even if Jesus is in your boat and you have asked the Lord into your heart, it won't always be sunshine, rainbows, and smooth sailing. Sometimes you can be close to him and still find yourself getting thrown around by the waves of life. So back to the story, this storm is rough, dudes are getting thrown all over the boat, they think they're about to die. And where do we find our hero? Asleep. Yes. Jesus is sleeping in the middle of the storm. Let that sink in and speak to you. He calmly awoke and told the storm to cease. And it did. He wasn't worried about perishing like the others were. He was relaxed and chilling knowing there was nothing to be afraid of. We may get soaked, but we are never sunk. So next time the waves seem too big and you think your ship is going down, before you panic, go wake up Jesus and let him do his thing. And when I say that, I don't intend for you to picture him asleep for lack of caring but rather he is asleep because he knows there is nothing to worry about. He has everything under control. He comes in clutch. He's like Derek Jeter that way. He shines brightest when the stage is biggest. Shout out to the captain.

CHAPTER FIFTEEN

Selling God

We've all seen them. The pastors everyone loves to hate. The guys who get on TV and tell you that if you "sow a seed" into their ministry, God will honor that and double, triple, heck, if he really loves you, quadruple it! Oh, you're sick? Well if you act now and sow a seed of $100, it will compel God to act and heal you. Sounds like a pretty sweet deal. I'm not going to name any names but I'm sure you can think of a few. I've fallen victim to this myself, this concept of buying God. I've seen it first hand, people with incurable illnesses and people thousands of dollars in debt, give thousands of dollars, sometimes giving money they currently did not have, money that could've paid bills, in order to get God's attention and ultimately his blessings. I absolutely believe God still heals but through prayer, not by checks in the offering bucket. I've seen tithes and offerings taken up three, sometimes four times a service, each one with a new promise of blessings, both financial and physical. I used to drink the Kool-Aid, thinking that if I just gave enough money, things would turn around. The more I give, the more God will give me. But hold on. Is that biblical? Yes, paying your tithes is biblical. Jesus said give Caesar his and give God his. Pay your bills, pay your tithes. Well, what about "planting a seed?" What about giving more and more money with the goal of getting more and more in return. The Bible says, those who bless others will themselves be blessed. This implies, giving, but it says nothing about expecting anything in return. This implies giving out of a pure heart. Giving is a biblical concept. We see it a lot in scripture and we see God honoring that. So it would make sense that the more you give, the more you get, but not quite. We give out of obedience to God and in order to help others. God will not honor selfishness.

God does not care if you drive a new Cadillac. This concept of buying God's blessings can often snowball into another fallacy preached today, and that is that as a Christian you should expect to be millionaires, and that it is God's will for you to be a millionaire and to live in a huge house, drive a luxury car, and be prosperous. I have actually been in a service where the pastor said, "All you young people come up to the altar. Everybody extend your hands toward these people. We're going to agree in prayer that all these young people become millionaires and marry tens (in reference to the scale one uses to judge the hotness of the opposite sex)." I don't have enough pages in this book to break down everything wrong with that statement. I mean, it says in the Bible that he has plans to prosper you. Does that mean financially? Does God want me to have a trophy wife? Does God care about how much money I make? Hebrews 13:5 says, "Keep your life free from love of money, and be content with what you have, for he has said, 'I will never leave you nor forsake you.'" (ESV). If we believe what the scripture says, then we have our answer right there. God isn't worried about money. So should we? Of course we should be responsible and pay our bills, but is it responsible or biblical to think the more we give, the more it will incline God to heal you or get you out of debt? No. Is it biblical to go to your local Cadillac dealership and claim one in the name of Jesus? Probably not.

Material wealth is cheap. Wealth will eventually pass away. You'll be gone one day and you can't take all your stuff with you. Money won't help you when you're struggling internally, fighting off your personal demons. Money can't always help when you hit a storm, and money cannot buy you freedom from addiction. What can, is a personal relationship with Jesus. I feel that in the prosperity mindset, it's preached you can give some money, and God is obligated to jump into action on your behalf, completely bypassing the meaning of Christianity, which is to know Jesus. Knowing Jesus is eternal life. And eternal life doesn't just mean in Heaven, eternal life starts now. Things of this world will pass away and money may be able to allow you to live to hold onto them a little longer but a relationship with Jesus is eternal.

―― CHAPTER SIXTEEN ――

Finding Jesus in the Dish Room

I do not know you. I do not know your story. I do not know your struggle. I do not know all that you've been through. Maybe life's been easy so far. Maybe it's been everything but. I do not know. But Jesus knows. Not only does he know, he cares. Despite what you know, or what you think you may know, despite the stereotypes and misfortunes that befall us here in this life, the love that Jesus has for you will never waiver. His love is so immense that he died for you. Romans 5:8 says, "But God shows his love for us in that while we were still sinners, Christ died for us." (ESV). God loves you so much that he sent his one and only son to die so that whosoever believes in him could have eternal life according to John 3:16. He didn't die so that all the religious people could have eternal life. He didn't die so just the "good" people could have eternal life. He died so whoever believes in him can have eternal life in Heaven. He died so that the broken, the messed up, the outcasts, the heartbroken could know what real love is by showing us *who* love is. God continues to move in our lives and sometimes the doors that open and shut aren't necessarily the ones we ourselves would have chosen.

Sometimes our circumstances will not reflect our faith, but we should always reflect our faith despite our circumstances. Things won't always make sense; life won't always make sense. But our concern as believers should be to follow the good shepherd even though everything else in this world is constantly competing for our attention. Worry will always be trying to get your attention. So will anger and jealousy. Unhappiness will try to creep into your life. Things will not always go according to plan, and you cannot help that, but you can choose, like Paul, to deny yourself, and put aside your own selfishness for the sake of proclaiming the Gospel. This life is not about us. This life is not about satisfying our desires. This life is not about having a spotlight on us and our accomplishments. This life we have been graciously given is about moving the spotlight off of us and pointing it on Jesus and what he has done for us. I found that Jesus is always present, not just in church but in conversations, life experiences, testimonies, and tears. I knew of Jesus from church, but I found him in the dish room.

About the Author

Schuyler Vowell lives in Mayfield, Kentucky. He loves sports and played college football for a short time before injuries ended his career, allowing him to find his true calling. He answered the call to the ministry at the age of eighteen and has been chasing God ever since. Schuyler is the founder and pastor of LOVE MKY Campus Ministry, a Christ-centered ministry geared toward influencing the culture while reaching the campus of Murray State University where he currently attends and majors in Organizational Communication and minors in Religious Studies. He no longer washes dishes. He makes burritos now. Follow him on Twitter @dishboypreacher and follow LOVE MKY on Instagram @love_mky.